AMELIA EDWARDS

AMELIA EDWARDS
Traveller, Novelist & Egyptologist

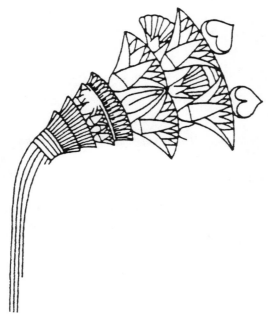

JOAN REES

The Rubicon Press

The Rubicon Press
57 Cornwall Gardens
London SW7 4BE

© Joan Rees, 1998

British Library Cataloguing-in-Publication Data.

A catalogue record for this book is available from the British Library.

0-948695-61-7 (hardback edition)
0-948695-60-9 (paperback edition)

Printed and bound in Great Britain by Biddles Limited of Guildford
and King's Lynn

Contents

List of Illustrations

For David and Elin

Acknowledgements

I am grateful to the following for access to the materials in their care and for permission to quote from them: the Principal and Fellows of Somerville College, Oxford; the Committee of the Egypt Exploration Society; the Librarian, University College London; Macclesfield Borough Council/Macclesfield Museums Trust; The Record Office, City of Bristol.

Introduction

Most of those to whom Amelia Edwards's name is familiar know her as an Egyptologist and the author of *A Thousand Miles up the Nile*. First published in 1877, this account of her visit to Egypt in 1873-4 has twice been reprinted in recent years. Mountain climbing enthusiasts know her earlier book, *Untravelled Peaks and Unfrequented Valleys*, which describes what she calls "a ramble" in the Dolomites at a time when that area of Italy was known to few foreigners. This book also has been reprinted to cater for appreciative modern readers. To those with more than a passing interest in Ancient Egypt Amelia Edwards is familiar as the moving spirit behind the foundation of the Egypt Exploration Society which for more than a hundred years has been devoted to excavation and preservation of the historic remains. In this cause she wrote innumerable articles for British and American periodicals. She was also the author of eight novels and many short stories: her ghost stories in particular have their devotees and are represented in recent anthologies.

These achievements are good reason for paying attention to Amelia Edwards both because of their intrinsic interest and because of what lies behind them. She was one of the brave company of nineteenth century women who carved out independent careers for themselves and she succeeded in exerting over one area - egyptology - an influence whose impetus is still felt. How her efforts bore upon her and what motivated and sustained them are questions worth asking. Even though answers necessarily remain tentative, exploration of the evidence and assessment of probabilities is still worth undertaking, for the personality of Amelia Edwards is a fascinating one and her career and its background in her personal life touch upon many issues active in the nineteenth century and still alive to-day.

Her story hinges on two climactic periods, the 1850's when she was in her early twenties and the winter of 1873-4 when she visited Egypt. The first set her on course for her career as novelist and journalist and the second led her to abandon fiction and to reorient her whole life. Biographical material is to be found mainly in the archives of the Egypt Exploration Society and in the library of Somerville College, Oxford. This, together with contemporary notices and two short autobiographical essays which Amelia wrote towards the end of her life, enable the essential background to be pieced together but there are areas which remain tantalisingly obscure. There is something enigmatic and impenetrable about Amelia Edwards, a sense that there is more in her make-up than lies on the surface. Wilful, unpredictable and daring as a girl, she grew into a brilliant young woman of energy and talent who, it seemed, might have done anything. In her middle years she became an adventurous traveller and a popular writer. In her early fifties she was transformed into a woman who was chained to her desk working from morning to night and sometimes through the night, writing up reports, composing articles, corresponding with scholars, soliciting funds and cultivating public interest in Egyptian antiquity by whatever means she could. She, who as a girl provoked anxiety among her staider relatives as they wondered what mischief she might be up to next, became in middle age a fount of soothing, smoothing emollience among the competing personalities and ambitions that grew evermore enflamed as the newly opened field of egyptology provided both opportunities and frustrations.

Age brings its changes but natural process does not quite account for Amelia Edwards. On the surface she is the most open and companionable of writers but from the time of her early maturity there are hints and suggestions that more goes on beneath the surface than the world is allowed to see. She presents herself as quite transparent but the claim is not convincing. "A literal unvarnished narrative" is her description of *A Thousand Miles up the Nile* but anything other than a casual glance shows at once that this is not so. *A Thousand Miles* is in fact a highly worked and extremely skilful exercise in the management of very varied materials ranging from the light-hearted to the intellectually demanding. Cohesion and acceptability are achieved by the invention of an author persona who is and is not Amelia Edwards herself. Some words with which she closes the preface to *A Thousand Miles* may aptly be turned to apply to her. Reproducing an image of the Sphinx from a painting by an old friend, Elihu Vedder, she comments: "It tells its own tale or rather it tells as much of its own tale as the artist chooses". As often happens in reading Amelia Edwards it is impossible to be sure whether she is writing in all innocence without any undercurrent of suppressed meaning or whether she smiled to herself as she wrote, knowing very well that she too, with all her apparent openness, told only so much of her own tale as she, "the artist", chose.

Her post-Egypt career has led attention away from the early years and obscured entirely her career as a novelist. Mrs Oliphant, Mrs Braddon, Mrs Lynn Linton and many others find a place in histories of nineteenth century fiction but Amelia Edwards does not. Contemporaries, however, counted her among the others. She was nothing like as prolific as many but her carefully worked novels were read with pleasure and respect and their distinctiveness was recognised. To a modern reader with the determination to get hold of them they come as something of a surprise. Of course they belong to their time but they are less "Victorian" as that quality is commonly understood than many of the better known names. Amelia Edwards makes forays into unconventional territory, she expresses - or at any rate hints at - advanced views, she encompasses surprisingly "unfeminine" material - students' drinking haunts in Paris, the ranks of red caps fighting for Italian independence, blockade-running in the American Civil War. She fills her books with reflections on art and with information on virtually every subject under the sun: the origins and language of the Etruscan people, the theory of evolution, fine wines, Italian dialects...the list could go on and on. She has also a keen line in satire and focuses a sharp eye on society manners. Competent in caricature and prolific in story invention, she is weak at character development through narrative but there are interesting things in all the novels and sometimes the writing is very accomplished indeed.

There will be an attempt in what follows to give the fiction the consideration it deserves and the novels will be read also for the light they throw on Amelia Edwards's life and character. They offer glimpses of events and reactions, ideas and inclinations for which other evidence is lacking and they allow for a more intimate portrait than is otherwise obtainable. The early novels are particularly revealing and among them especially *Hand and Glove*. The interrelation of life and novels makes clear distinction between biography and literary criticism difficult and the two approaches are to some extent intertwined throughout this study but in chapter IV the fiction is brought together for discussion in its own terms and an assessment of its qualities, its merits and demerits is attempted.

The endeavour of the book as a whole is to bring into the light a very accomplished writer, a woman whose multiple talents fed two careers and whose character, elusive and fascinating, is of compelling interest.

Amelia Blandford Edwards, known to family and friends as Amy, was born on June 7th, 1831, at no.1, Westmoreland Place, City Road, Islington. Her father, Thomas, had served under Wellington in the Peninsular War but ill-health had obliged him to retire and in civilian life he supplemented his diminished income with a job in the London and Westminster Bank. His family were gentlemen farmers in Suffolk. His wife, Alicia, came from a family closely related to the Fitzgeralds and other old Irish families. Her father was Robert, a barrister, the last male representative of the Irish branch of the Norfolk family of Walpoles. Thomas and Alicia had been married in County Sligo in 1816, he then forty-three and she thirty. Amelia, their only child, was born fifteen years later.

Thomas Edwards evidently pined for his military life and tried to reproduce as a civilian the regularity and discipline of the army. His days followed an unvarying and strictly timed programme according to which he read *The Times*, breakfasted, went to the Bank, returned, took his evening meal and went to bed. He talked little and had no taste for outside company. When the Crimean War broke out he was in his sixties but he offered his services to the War Office as one "able and willing to serve". The unrealistic offer shows well enough where his heart lay.

Alicia Edwards made up amply for her husband's lack of sprightliness for she was a lively and intelligent woman with interests well beyond the domestic hearth. She took charge of the greater part of Amelia's education though a governess and, later, masters were also employed. Always an independent student, far more receptive to what she taught herself than to instruction by others, Amelia was lucky that her parents were enlightened enough to allow her free rein to read anything that came her way. Mrs Edwards was herself a great reader and her example encouraged Amelia to read abundantly. Travel books particularly delighted her and in later years she had vivid memory of the enjoyment with which, as a very small child, she "devoured" Sir John Gardner Wilkinson's *Manners and Customs of the Ancient Egyptians* and Stephens's *Central America*.

Though money was tight and Mr Edwards did not share her taste, his wife indulged a passion for the theatre and went frequently to Sadlers Wells. Amelia accompanied her and imbibed a life-long love of the drama from these early years. Mrs Edwards emerges as a woman with an unusually broad-minded view of the proper education of young girls. Young Amy was allowed to feed her mind on the drama and on whatever books she chose and also, a negative freedom, she was not burdened with domestic tasks. Her mother was herself a careful housekeeper since economy was required in this far from affluent family but Amelia was never called upon for even the most ordinary duties. Years later she would surprise landladies in the Dolomites by being able to make an omelette, an accomplishment not expected of the well-to-do English lady she had then, by her efforts, become: but this far from advanced accomplishment stemmed from her traveller's resourcefulness rather than from anything she learned at her mother's knee. Household skills, Mrs Edwards evidently felt, could be left to ordinary girls and she saw promise in her Amy that destined her for more ambitious things. Her attitude was not common at her time or later as witness, for example, the Amy of Louisa M. Alcott's *Little Women* who herself showed some signs of artistic talent in her childhood but who declares, when her daughter looks as though she may have inherited the gift, that she is more proud of the pricks in the child's finger made by her baby efforts to learn to sew than she is of her childish paintings and drawings. Mrs Edwards on the contrary fostered Amelia's talents by every means she could and encouraged her to have pride and confidence in herself.

If her initial wish was to bring her daughter up to supply the companionship her husband did not offer, she had every reason to feel her hopes more than met, for Amelia gave signs very early of being remarkably talented. At the age of four she wrote a story and, since she could not manage joined-up writing, she printed it all in capitals. At seven she had a poem, "The Knights of Old", published in a penny weekly and a little later she contributed stories to similar publications. At twelve she was writing freely and a talent for drawing had developed to such an extent that a sketch of hers on the back of a short story which she had boldly submitted caught the eye of the celebrated artist, George Cruikshank, who edited the journal. Unaware of her age, he called at the house to meet the talented author and artist and was surprised and greatly amused to find that the person he sought was a little girl. He offered to take her as his pupil and train her in his own profession but her parents, prejudiced against the artist-life, demurred and the opportunity slipped by.

In her mid-teens she decided to concentrate all her energies on music and for some seven years, from fourteen to twenty-one, she studied hard, practising at times for as much as eight hours a day, teaching as well as taking lessons. She composed copiously and became a skilled performer. She had besides a good singing voice.

It was no wonder that the mother was filled with pride in her multi-talented daughter but the consequences were not always entirely comfortable for others. Young Amelia was spirited, full of energy and, as "the personification of fun and childish daring" according to her cousin, Matilda Betham-Edwards, she could be unruly. She and her mother spent summer holidays in the country at the farmhouse home of Uncle Henry and Aunt Betsy at Baylham in the Suffolk countryside where her father's roots were. A family of seven cousins, including Matilda, lived at Westerfield Hall nearby and in this company and this environment the young Amelia had unrestricted scope for her high spirits. Home life was constrained and she saw very little of other children. She seized her freedom in Suffolk eagerly but not without cost to relatives who were in a constant state of alarm as to what she would get up to next - opening the tap on a barrel of harvest beer so that half of it was lost before anyone discovered what she had done - a serious loss for the beer was a highly prized item in the farming community; or locking a rather fussy maiden aunt in the pantry. She had charm then as she had throughout her life and the more pranks she played, the more charming she became and the more she won hearts. Her mother was tireless in singing her praises and boasting of her accomplishments and so excited by her gifted child that she could not restrain her enthusiasm even in Amelia's own presence. Overwhelmed by the combination of mother and daughter, aunts and uncles and cousins alike were inhibited from applying the usual strictures to so exceptional a child. She got away with more than perhaps she should and the adulation and indulgence might well have ruined her character. She appears to have emerged unspoilt but this childhood, with its high expectations and its adoring mother, left a mark on her adult life.

Love of Suffolk remained with her and she used it as a background for happy childhood years in *Barbara's History* (1864), the novel which she counted as the first of her maturity and with which she made her name.

One physical evidence of her talents at that time was a mural she did on the whitewashed walls of a room in the farm at Creeting St Peter's where Uncle William and Aunt Maria lived. It was designed to be some six foot square and its subject was "The Landing of the Romans in Britain." The mural survived for many years, a piece notable mainly for the graphic drawing in the foreground of bodies being trampled under foot and of an axe-wielding semi-naked Briton about to smite a well-accoutred and remarkably static Roman, none other than Julius Caesar himself. It is not a work which promises genius though it is well composed and shows skill with the pencil - or in this instance chalk. It is certainly not a pretty, lady-like production but rather the work of a vigorous and confident young artist whose imagination is gripped by dramatic and even violent scenes.

6

Amelia's artistic skills remained with her all her life and she made good use of them in illustrating her travel books.

As for the theatre, Amelia was not content to be merely a member of an audience. In her twenties acting was a passion she delighted to indulge and she was a leading performer in family theatricals. Her musical voice and her clear enunciation were part of her equipment as an actress as later they were of her success as a lecturer. If the stage had been a more respectable career for a well-brought up young woman perhaps she would have followed it. As it was, display of her talents had to be confined to family and friends, not always in a theatrical setting. At twenty-two she had not outgrown her capacity for pranks and one day with the connivance of a male cousin she dressed up as a young man just arrived from London and presented herself with a letter of introduction to the Suffolk relations. She was remarkably convincing in her male role.

At about this time she wrote what she called "a dramatic entertainment" entitled *Home and Foreign Lyrics*. This consisted of character impersonations and song. Performed by Miss Julia St. George, a well known figure of the time, it toured the country and ran, according to Amelia's own testimony, for many years. It is referred to in a foot-note to the novel, *The Ladder of Life* (1857) and Amelia was evidently proud of it.

Personal attractiveness, many talents and a loving family: the wind seemed to be set fair for Amelia but everything was not such plain sailing as might appear. The family moved to a better house in Wharton Street, Percy Circus, Amelia perhaps contributing to the family budget since her career as a writer was by that time under way. In some late autobiographical notes she ascribes to an "accident" the decision to make writing her career or "new trade" as she calls it: a short story written in "an idle moment" during a summer holiday - the first literary effort since her childhood days - was accepted by a magazine and earned her a cheque; so she wrote another and followed it with essays and articles. Twelve months' continued success and the cheques which went with it persuaded her that this was in future to be her métier; but the choice was not arrived at painlessly. Reflecting on Cruikshank's offer of an apprenticeship and the failure to take it up, Amelia wondered long afterwards if indeed she had missed her vocation at that time. She had wanted to be an artist. To be a professional illustrator would have been at least half way to fulfilling her ambition and clearly some bitterness still lingers that she was denied the life in art which had been her wish. The odd objection had been made that she was "too delicate to paint in oils" and she had taken this as putting out of reach the excellence she aspired to. The memory of that dampener was certainly with her when she wrote *Barbara's History*. Barbara's step-mother remarks that she has heard that "oils are sometimes bad for the chest".

Barbara laughs at this and adds "I scarcely knew why". No explanation is offered in the text but the reference had a meaning, albeit a somewhat caustic one, for Amelia.

In fact, however ill-founded their objection to oil-painting may have been, Amelia's parents had reason to be concerned about her health and a delicate childhood was capped by a severe attack of typhoid fever throughout the winter of 1849.

A career in art denied her, Amelia first turned to music and worked at that with the determination and concentration that always characterised her. A compelling urge to achieve more than mere competence drove her through her marathon programme of study and practice even though, as she afterwards wrote, she was "by no means passionately fond of music". She thought at one time of becoming a professional singer and early success in a concert filled her with excitement and hope. Disaster struck, however, in the form of a series of colds and sore throats and she was obliged to break an engagement to sing in oratorio at Exeter Hall. Disgusted and disappointed she gave up the idea and concentrated instead on possibilities as an instrumentalist. In 1850 she became organist at St Michael's Church, Wood Green, a new church near Wharton Street, and she sought testimonials from distinguished performers which might enable her to establish a career. Sir John Goss, organist at St Paul's Cathedral, wrote in September 1852 that she had played for him a prelude and fugue of her own composition "in a very creditable manner". Matilda Betham-Edwards gives a less cautious account of Amelia's style. On one of Amelia's visits to Suffolk with her mother she played the organ for the service at Witnesham Church and Matilda writes:

> I well remember how she varied the cut and dry programme, and how the congregation lingered spell-bound at the close of the service. She was playing us out with a voluntary of Bach's, but nobody stirred till the magic notes ceased. Music of this impassioned kind was a novelty to the naive listeners.

Creditable or impassioned, Amelia's music would not do. It was "an evil hour" when she first turned to it, she wrote; the seven teenage years she gave to it were "virtually thrown away" and she seems never to have forgiven the "waste".

Music features with more or less prominence in two of her novels. *The Ladder of Life* of 1857 is set in Freibourg, a city which Amelia had visited, probably for the sake of the famous organ which features in the novel. The heroine is befriended by Mr Vaughan, himself an organist and also eventually a successful opera-composer. Among her many adventures she is persecuted by the attentions of a mad Italian violinist and she becomes a renowned singer though she gives up her career on marriage. The hero of *Debenham's Vow* (1870) is a parish organist before he embarks on an exotic career abroad. In spite of its role in these books, however - and in *Debenham's Vow* it is very slight - music never has the same place in Amelia's writing as art does. References to works of art and discussions of practice and theory occur frequently but there are very few occasions when music is evoked. The failure of ambition and time fruitlessly spent left a sore place and she avoided it.

So finally she turned to the third talent, writing. She joined the staff of the *Saturday Review* and the *Morning Post* and became a successful journalist who covered everything in the course of her career except Parliament and police reports. More immediately, between 1855 and 1858 she produced a clutch of publications: *My Brother's Wife: A Life History* in 1855; *A Summary of English History* in 1856; *The Ladder of Life: A Heart History* and *The Young Marquis: or a Story from a Reign* in 1857; *Hand and Glove: a Tale* and *The History of France* in 1858. The historical compilations are evidently publishers' fodder, useful means of keeping the wolf from the door. The fiction points to the road she was to pursue with increasing success for nearly twenty years.

The arduous work of the 1850's was Amelia's second attempt to lay the foundations of a career. She had failed in music but she was to succeed in literature: hindsight should not obscure the fact that it must have been an anxious time, fraught with stress of more than one kind. She may or may not have been naturally ambitious but her childhood and upbringing were such as to develop a strong sense of obligation to distinguish herself. Her mother's pride and the admiration of relatives imposed a duty to be brilliant and it was one that she embraced willingly enough. Hard work was never a disincentive but as she entered her twenties she was becoming aware that there were obstacles which would not yield to determination and endeavour. Her talent for music was, it seemed, not great enough, her enthusiasm for art was not matched, so she was told, by her physical fitness; and if either of these impediments had been minimised or removed, there remained the fact that she was a woman and for a woman to aspire to an independent, let alone a distinguished, career in the 1840's and '50's was to challenge social forces that were all but overwhelming. Whether or not Amelia's confidence was shaken, her parents must have felt real anxiety. Their discouragement of her artistic aspirations may have stemmed from other things than uncertainty about her strength. Doubts of the morality of artists' studios perhaps had something to do with it and, besides, there was a prudential consideration. Recognition for women artists and access to professional bodies was an aspect of female emancipation which had to be hard fought for and was long in coming. Music, on the other hand, might seem to offer better prospects as singer, performer and teacher and hope as well as money would have been invested in the seven long years of preparation for a career which in the end did not so much as begin.

As elderly parents Thomas and Alicia had special reason to be anxious about future provision for their only child and in all likelihood it is their worry on her behalf which explains an engagement which she entered into in January 1851. The gentleman's name was Bacon and, whatever his merits may have been, Amelia was so far from loving him that she seems even to have felt positive aversion: the walk home from church with him every Sunday was a weekly encounter looked forward to with dread. Worse still, the engagement was a fatal obstruction to the development of another attachment, to an Irish cousin. There is no clue to his identity. Mrs Edwards had taken Amelia to Ireland in 1841 and there, revelling in the beautiful countryside and with greater freedom than at home, Amelia enjoyed herself hugely. If she met the cousin then she would have been too young to form an attachment and when he appeared in London in 1851 she may not have known him well. Of his frustrated intentions she says only that "my unfortunate engagement prevented this chance". Cousin Matilda seems to be referring to this period and particularly to Mr Bacon when she writes with tantalising lack of specificity that Amelia possessed "the perilous dower of personal fascination. No one ever exercised stronger influence, and it was hardly her fault if she at times awakened interest or affection she could not return." Matilda is not always an accurate chronicler but clearly she had heard something about at least one distressing entanglement.

Not surprisingly given all the circumstances, Amelia in 1851 was miserable, lonely and ill, her physical condition then as at other points in her life reflecting her miserable state of mind. Then she made a break. She gave up music and she gave up Mr Bacon. She embarked seriously on her writing and it brought her money and the promise of success. It was time for the past to be put aside: the future was still to make.

Up to this point she had been home-based but that was to change. She went to Paris in 1853 and again in 1854. She began to correspond with a Frenchman, Emile Stéger, who became "the dearest and most intimate of friends". Every Tuesday she would walk down the road to meet the postman bringing Stéger's letters and every Wednesday she replied to them . She met him in Paris in 1855 and with one or two other friends they talked, smoked, drank champagne and she was "thoroughly happy". Stéger was perhaps more important to her than either Mr Bacon or the Irish cousin but after the joyous summer of 1855 he drops out of the story. From Paris Amelia went on to explore France further - whether or not

Stéger was still in the party is unclear - and acquired incidentally that connoisseur's knowledge of wines and vintages which is displayed in several of her novels. The travels extended into Germany and Switzerland before she returned again to England. During this period she took up pistol-shooting and riding and even tried her hand at oil painting, evidently throwing off ill health and fears of it at the same time as she burst out of the restricted environment of her earlier years into the freedom of continental life and congenial companionship. Just so, as a child, she had burst out with disconcertingly high spirits whenever she was released into the freedom of Suffolk and the stimulus of company of her own age.

In 1855 her first novel, *My Brother's Wife*, was published and reviewers acknowledged the presence of a new talent on the literary scene. With the success of the book the crisis was over which had begun with her failure to find a niche in music. The course now set was to hold steady until with the second determining moment of her life - the voyage to Egypt in 1873 - she once more reordered her life and changed her direction.

II

The novel which follows *My Brother's Wife* is not in itself promising. The *Ladder of Life* of 1857 is a fantastic assemblage of kidnapping, pursuit by a deranged lover, attempted assault and the miraculous discovery of a superlative singing voice - to mention only a few of its ingredients. The relation to Amelia's actual experience is minimal but as a revelation of her inner life at the time the book has value. It leaves no doubt of the highly-coloured spectacles through which she chose to look at life and the career of the heroine, Natalie, she of the remarkable voice, is evidently a wish-fulfilment fantasy. Natalie climbs the ladder from street-singer to performer in a travelling company - like Miss Julia St.George's - thence to the Drury Lane chorus and finally to replacing the prima donna in the principal role in an opera. She becomes overnight a great star. Then a young hero arrives from Switzerland and love sweeps all before it. Perhaps this was wish-fulfilment too. Natalie promptly gives up her career because Laurent would not like her to appear on the stage. None of Amelia's heroines in any of her novels is allowed to pursue an independent career but the claims of a woman's talents are never brushed aside quite so casually again. The fact is that the hectic events of *The Ladder of Life* preclude serious thought about anything but, such as it is, the novel is a piquant indication of the young Amelia's zest for strongly spiced experience.

Such experience may have remained in the realm solely of the imagination but there is reason to believe that she really did make bold forays beyond the usual barriers. Details of Amelia's life in the fifties and sixties are hard to come by but, in the absence of independently attested facts, the novels provide an alternative means of access to the shape and character of those years. *The Ladder of Life* contributes something and *In the Days of my Youth*, a novel of 1873, provides more. In this novel the young hero, Basil, goes to Paris in the late 40's/early 50's to study medicine. He falls in with other students, mainly artists, and acquires an extensive knowledge of the topography of Paris and of the Bohemian life. The chapters devoted to this contribute nothing to narrative development but in themselves they are lively and entertaining. The shop talk and ribaldry of the students in their favourite haunts, the vaudeville theatre they frequent and the entertainment there - all is given in detail and with relish. The old Latin Quarter in particular is evoked with warmth and nostalgia. Even sexual activity is not entirely ignored and Amelia goes out of her way to make an affectionate defence of the grisettes who were indispensable features of the settings in which the students lived their lives. The question arises: how did Amelia come by her knowledge of the places and manners of a way of life which was overwhelmingly masculine and certainly not open to middle class English ladies? That the students are art students is easily enough understood given Amelia's predilections. To imitate with some vivacity their conversation and to envisage their various types in vivid physical detail was well within her capacity but even so she needed models to work from. Certainly the intimacy with which she describes the locations, including the seedy theatre, cannot but have been derived from personal knowledge.

It may have been Emile Stéger who introduced her to places she could never have got to on her own and perhaps, to make it easier, he helped, as a cousin had done at Westerfield, to pass her off as a man. George Sand was a blazing light in those days. Amelia knew her work well - there are several laudatory references in *Hand and Glove* (1858) - and it would be surprising if she and her books were not among the subjects covered either in the letters exchanged with Stéger or in the hours they spent together in Paris. George Sand with her cigars and her trousers and her free way of life showed that a woman could release herself from conventions and claim a right to a wider experience than society in general was ready to countenance. Though Amelia's English upbringing would never have allowed her to follow the whole way, George Sand's example was an encouragment to cross at least some barriers. Amelia was young and at liberty for the first time to be and do whatever she dared. She was moreover a good actress and with some discreet support could well have been passed off as a young man. Cross-dressing was not unknown even in London and *The Times* reported in 1868 that some women had dressed as men to go to the theatre and to enter "a famous London club". In an album in Somerville College, Oxford, there is a curious photograph of Lucy Renshawe, later to be Amelia's companion in the Dolomites and in Egypt, in which she appears with severely cropped hair and wearing a cravat and a masculine jacket. The photographer has even brushed in shadows along her cheeks to represent sideboards! The photograph may have been merely a joke but perhaps it indicates that Amelia and Lucy Renshawe embarked for a time on a relatively serious campaign to test the liberating effects of masculine attire.

Amelia's knowledge of the Parisian art world need not have depended on Stéger. In an account of herself written near the end of her life she recalls with pride her long acquaintance with American artists of repute, Frederic Edwin Church, C.C.Coleman and Elihu Vedder. Coleman and Vedder in particular had strong connections with Europe. Coleman went to Paris in 1859 and after serving in the American Civil War returned to Europe and made his home in Capri. Vedder followed the same pattern. He lived in France from 1856-61 and after war years in America he returned to settle finally in Italy. He made his home in Rome but spent summers in Capri. Acquaintance with these men and others of their ilk, young like her in their Parisian days, would familiarise Amelia with artists' studios and it is not at all unlikely that they smuggled her into the clubs. Amelia was always keen to see for herself and second-hand accounts would only have whetted her curiosity, not satisfied it.

When *In the Days of My Youth* was reviewed in *The Saturday Review* the question of how much Amelia had seen for herself much exercised the reviewer. He is divided between reproaching Amelia for writing about things of which she is necessarily ignorant and the shocked thought on the edge of his mind that somehow or other perhaps she did know the scenes she describes. He is particularly appalled that a woman should have a good word to say for grisettes: there would be no objection, he says, if it had come from a man.

If daring did take Amelia to the men's clubs, it may have led her to make an even more audacious entry into the male world. Basil and his friend Muller go to Molino's, a public baths for men, and there observe male bodies in various forms of undress and nakedness. Basil recognises one, "a tall young man, an elegant of the first water, a curled darling of society, a professed lady-killer...He now looked like a monkey". "Gracious heavens!", Basil exclaims, "What would become of the world if clothes went out of fashion?" "Humph!", Muller replies, "one half of us, my dear fellow, would commit suicide." There could be a literary origin for this, Carlyle's mischievous proposal in *Sartor Resartus* (1833) to imagine the House of Lords in their nakedness, but Amelia is not at the moment interested in the social and political implications of Carlylean nudity. It is the physical appearance which takes all her attention and she does not mince matters in giving her verdict. Fat, thin, old, young, bow-legged, knock-kneed, short, tall, brown, yellow, "some got up for effect in gorgeous wrappers; and all more or less hideous" - the male specimens gathered at Molino's leave her, to say the least, unimpressed.

Amelia had longed to be an artist especially to be a figure painter and to study from life. Though she renounced the ambition, she never ceased to sketch, to paint water-colours and use an artist's eye. If she persuaded her male companions to take her to the public baths as a man it would have been as an artist that she wanted to go. Women got a foot in the door of the Royal Academy schools in 1860 when Laura Herford submitted her drawings signed only with the initial L. and was admitted before it was realised that she was of the forbidden sex; but across the threshold there were further barriers and women were excluded from Life Classes. Amelia, if she went through the door at Molino's, was snapping her fingers at all conventions, restrictions and prejudices. In the baths she could study as many models as she cared to and the result, as it turned out, was to confirm the direction in which she had impressed Cruikshank as a child. Late in life she confessed to being still a caricaturist though, with the self-protective prudence which grew upon her as years passed, she kept to herself the drawings which would have betrayed that the mild mannered and conciliatory Miss Edwards, as she was then, observed the world in fact with a sharp satiric eye.

Everything that is known of the early life of Amelia Edwards points to her as a high-spirited young woman looking for the ladder by which, like her heroine Natalie, she could climb to eminence. She needed an outlet for her gifts and for the energies which led her to explore unconventional paths in diverse directions. One small snippet of biographical information helps to confirm and fill out the picture. Her artistic connections, it would appear, brought her into circles which were not only bohemian in behaviour but radical in politics. The painter, Samuel Laurence, gathered round him in his studio in London a phalanstery, or group in sympathy with the ideas of the French socialist thinker, Charles Fourier. As well as writers and artists, the company included well-known public figures, among them Robert Owen, remembered for his efforts to give practical form to his theories of social reform, and Matilda Hays who planned to translate George Sand into English. The novelist, Eliza Lynn Linton, an agnostic in religion and described by her recent biographer as a "communist" in politics, was of the number and so was Amelia Edwards. Hints in several novels suggest that she had a sharp sense of social inequalities and even nursed republican sympathies but it is rare to find evidence of Amelia joining a group of any kind: all the more striking, then, her inclusion in Laurence's distinguished phalanstery.

Her life in these years was a rich mix of travel, experiment and adventure and contact with men and women outside the conventional pale. One fruit of her willingness to break bounds in thought as well as action is the novel *Hand and Glove*. *Hand and Glove* (1858) is worth attention on several counts but above all for the character of the Reverend Alexis Hamel, a Protestant priest newly arrived in Chalons-sur-Saône: this is an area which had been on Amelia's route in her travels of 1855. Hamel is about forty years of age and of a strikingly handsome and impressive appearance. He takes as his text on the first Sunday "Think not that I am come to send peace on earth: I come not to send peace, but a sword" and he proceeds to deliver an astonishing sermon. It is a brilliantly caustic account of the history of Christianity in its darkest aspects - a "fearful tale of blood" in which "the faith, so often overborne by bloodshed, uprose and triumphed in bloodshed" and in which torture and wholesale killing were justified in the cause of saving souls. After eighteen centuries "of sorrow and suffering", he asks, has Christianity triumphed? "Are the nations convinced? Is the victory gained over ignorance, and indifference and idolatry? Alas, no. It is not gained. It never will be gained. It is the old struggle of the sea and the shore, and what is conquered on the one coast is reclaimed on the other." The followers of lies outnumber the faithful, as millions outnumber hundreds, and false gods prevail. The message is "'Despair, again I say, despair!'"

It is an extraordinarily powerful and damning piece of oratory delivered, as the first person narrator reports, with a rare and impassioned eloquence "supported by reading so extensive and judgement so keen". As she is leaving the church the narrator is asked her opinion. "M. Hamel's view of life and of Christianity does not please me. His sermon appeared to me more like a profound satire than a genuine lamentation", she replies; but if Hamel is, as she calls him, "'a sceptic at heart'" she herself has at least some affinity with him for she has already acknowledged that the sermon has sunk too deeply into her mind ever to be forgotten.

As for Amelia Edwards who wrote the sermon and who fails to repudiate its argument or its conclusion, the episode is one more proof that her willingness to defy orthodoxy went beyond adventures in Parisian clubs and public baths and that she was open to heterodox influence of all kinds. Mrs Linton's *Christopher Kirkland* made a similar attack on the works of Christianity in the *Autobiography* of 1885 but Amelia anticipates her by nearly thirty years. *Hand and Glove* does not turn on religious debate - that kind of intellectualising is not in her line - but Hamel's sermon is conspicuous evidence of the attractiveness to her of taboo territory at this time of her life.

The whole presentation of Hamel reinforces this idea. He is dazzlingly clever and multi-accomplished: a singer, a poet, a connoisseur of art of all kinds, a critic, a story-teller. All that he does he does with polish, charm and immense skill so that everyone else fades into nonentity and meanness compared with him. Immeasurably superior in intelligence to his company, he indulges a quiet irony which they fail to observe. He is also sexually far more attractive than the nominal hero to whom Marguerite has been contracted since she was thirteen. Hamel's power to rouse the still very young and innocent Marguerite is left in no doubt and equally clear is Charles's failure to do anything of the kind. (He wins the girl in the end but only when Hamel is removed). Two scenes, both turning on acts of cruelty, underline the contrast between the men and they speak unmistakably of the young Amelia's sexual awareness and her boldness in expressing it.

The first scene follows from Marguerite's disregard of a wish, strongly expressed by Charles and amounting in fact to an instruction, that she should read a book about Roman burial customs in preparation for a visit to a columbarium, or ancient burial site, which has been newly discovered in his grounds. His attitude towards her is invariably pedagogic. She resents it and, besides, she finds the book boring. When the visit takes place and she asks what is inside the jars she finds there, Charles sees that she has ignored him and, to punish her, he tells her to put her hand in one and find for herself what it contains. The shock of discovering that, as he coldly tells her, she is holding in her hand "the cinders of one who was once a being like yourself" sends her into hysterics and he has to woo her with apologies and sweetmeats before he can regain some favour.

The other scene is of quite a different character. It is full of sexual vibrations and anticipates D.H. Lawrence by some seventy years. Marguerite and her companion, Gartha, witness Hamel mercilessly beating his dog to compel obedience, just as Gudrun and Ursula watch Gerald Crich beat his mare in *Women in Love*. The Lawrence scene is incomparably the more powerful and significant but this should not obscure the original and daring nature of Amelia's achievement. She has perceived what psychologists of a later age have spelled out, the close connection between sex and sadism and in full consciousness, evidently, of what she is doing has expressed it by the sophisticated invention of the two complementary scenes. Both represent acts of male assertiveness and the urge to mastery. One is sexually charged and potent: "How pitiless he was", exclaims Marguerite later, "and yet there was something fine about it, after all!". Charles's brutality, on the other hand, is cerebral and cold. Emily Brontë perhaps inspired both the perception and the technique but the intelligence and the willingness to take risks remain whether the scenes are founded in personal observation or come through literature.

In spite of all his qualities Hamel is, as emerges at the end, a branded criminal, guilty of numerous acts of bad faith and illicit dealing. Unmasked as an escaped convict, he becomes a hunted man who dies in the end by his own hand, defeated and weary. He deserves a distinguished place among all those romantic heroes sired by Byron who are brilliant but blighted by dark secrets in their past. Hamel is more intellectual than most and he is analysed with subtlety by Amelia Edwards who is clearly herself fascinated by him. Even in his downfall she stresses his virtues: he was brave, he truly loved Marguerite, he could have been a great man if early circumstances had been different; those who expose him in the name of the law are not heroic or admirable but merely cold and unheroic personations of nemesis. Hamel is animated by the questioning, seeking spirit of his author, a young woman overflowing with mental and physical energy. He is not the last of his line but he is the most brilliant and the one who arouses in the mind of his creator fewer moral scruples and more admiration than his successors.

The glamour of Hamel's defiance of the world of bourgeois taste and convention is not sustained by those later figures who have some kinship with him. As Amelia worked into her literary career she became more self-conscious and more reserved and she set about constructing a persona behind which intimacies of feeling and opinion could be effectually hidden. An obvious motive was the need to avoid giving offence to the readers whom she needed for her livelihood but some deeper resistance to exposure may also have operated. The girl who, her cousin reports, threw a loaf of bread out of the nursery window for a bet and kept elderly relatives on tenterhooks is recognisable in the young woman who talked, smoked and adventured her way round Europe and also in the creator of Hamel. She is more difficult to find later.

III

The 50's saw Amelia given her head, seizing her freedom and beginning to express herself uninhibitedly, but as the new decade opened a severe shock was in store. On August 22nd, 1860, her father died of bronchitis at the age of seventy-two after a brief illness and Mrs Edwards died four days later of pneumonia. She was sixty. The sudden and unexpected loss, particularly of the mother to whom she had been so close at an age when she might expect her support and companionship for many more years, must have come as a staggering blow to Amelia. She may not have been very close to her taciturn, reclusive father but she was proud of his army career and in her own later life it became apparent that she inherited from him habits of regularity and self-discipline. Her ties with her mother were more emotional even to the extent, if cousin Matilda can be believed, that Amelia preserved to the very last a fragment of pastry from the last dish prepared for her by her doting parent.

Amelia later described the bereavements of this one week as "The great misfortune of my life" and this may not have been an exaggeration. The deaths came like a sudden blasting frost on a life just beginning to flower and from that time dates the loss of dash and brio of first youth and the more guarded presentation of herself and her ideas. There are no more overtly defiant gestures against propriety and orthodoxy. The spirit of questioning and challenge which bubbles into life in Paris and is expressed in *Hand and Glove* does not cease to exist but Amelia Edwards is no longer able confidently to display it.

Amelia's relationship with her mother never reached its natural adult conclusion. The umbilical cord was not cleanly cut by marriage and Amelia's career was not soundly enough established by the time of Mrs Edwards' death to give her a fully independent life of her own. Something like this seems to be the explanation for two events, one fictional and one real, which occur in following years. The fictional event occurs in the novel *Debenham's Vow* (1870) and takes the form of a late and unexpected development. The hero starts life living with his mother in Islington (where Amelia and her parents lived). He plays the organ in the parish church (as Amelia did). He dreams of making a name for himself as a musician (also as Amelia did) but the prospects are poor. Then his life changes abruptly and he is involved in a series of dramatic adventures in Italy and the southern states of America. He marries a cold-hearted beauty for her money but they have no sooner embarked on their honeymoon than he becomes ill. His wife softens in the experience of nursing him and she hopes that he will grow to love her as she begins to love him; but at this point his mother arrives at the foreign hotel where her son lies and at once takes charge of the nursing and resumes her old role as his principal companion and confidante. The wife is excluded and all prospect of a fulfilled marriage is destroyed.

In her twenties Amelia had thought about the cruelty which may underlie romance and now, approaching forty, she thought about mother love. Mrs Debenham, by her possessive devotion to her son, prevents him from forming a close relationship with any other woman: the infusion of this element into *Debenham's Vow*, treated as it is with considerably more psychological credibility than the novel as a whole, strongly suggests that Amelia was confronting what might be a truth about herself. The closeness of her relation with her mother may or may not have inhibited the development of a lasting bond with a man but fairly certainly it constituted an indispensable element in her life without which she seems hardly to have been able to function. Mother-dependency was deeply engrained in her for - the second and real life event - when Mrs Edwards died Amelia moved to another home and found another companion/mother. Though there was a disparity of thirty years in their ages, Amelia outlived this quasi-maternal figure by only a few months.

Mrs Emma Braysher who enters the story at this point, was born in 1804. Like Mrs Edwards she was interested in the theatre and had entertained the famous actor-manager Macready, among other "wits and celebrities" as Amelia says, at her table. She herself wrote poetry, at least in her youth. The Brayshers, in fact, appear to have been cultured people with a distinguished circle of acquaintances. Coleridge was writing to John Braysher, the husband, in 1818 asking him to help publicise his lectures and Mazzini wrote copiously to a Braysher daughter about Italy and Italian history, always sending regards to her mother. Mazzini's fight for Italian independence was much admired in England despite his strongly republican principles. The closeness of their association with him suggests that the Brayshers had rather more than the usual liberal sympathy with his ideas. Friendship between the Edwards and Braysher families - at least between the women folk - was close and Amelia was staying at the Brayshers' Kensington home in 1860 shortly before her parents' death. She may have moved in with them afterwards and it is probably in this period and under their patronage that she "went into society" with all that entailed of "dining, driving, dressing and the rest of it". Introduction to society under the wing of the Brayshers was a far cry from the life of the artists' quarters in Paris and Amelia developed no taste for it. She later described it as "treadmill work" but the experience contributed to the graceful social poise for which she was later notable. At the same time it gave her ammunition for the sardonic, even bitter, scenes of society life which recur in her novels.

Mr Braysher died in 1863 and the only surviving child, a daughter, followed him a year later. Amelia and Mrs Braysher, alike bereaved of their nearest and dearest, decided to repair their losses as best they might by making a home together. Harriet Mary Braysher had died in Bath and it was in the same area of Somerset that Mrs Braysher bought the house which she and Amelia were thenceforth to share for the rest of their lives. It was in Westbury-on-Trym, now a suburb of Bristol though it still retains reminders of its long history and of the quiet village it was in the nineteenth century. The house was called The Larches, and stood in Eastfield, a road which was then a narrow lane leading to fields and open country. It was destroyed by a direct hit during the second world war though the house next door still stands. Amelia boasted of the seclusion of The Larches, "quite away from the village, and surrounded by trees". For further protection from the outside world its acre of ground was closely walled in. It had originally been quite a small house but successive owners had enlarged it and over time Amelia and Mrs Braysher added their own quota of extensions and alterations. There Amelia lived and worked when she was at home, publishing a novel, *Half a Million of Money*, in 1865 and a book of ballads in the same year. She wrote many short stories, some of them for the Christmas numbers of Dickens's *Household Words* and *All the Year Round*. Two collections appeared, *Miss Carew* in 1865 and *Monsieur Maurice* in 1873. In 1870 *Debenham's Vow* was published and in 1873 *In the Days of my Youth*.

Amelia's life appeared to be in retreat, confined to her desk and to such of the local society of Westbury-on-Trym as were allowed to penetrate the solitude of The Larches. Later on this would by and large be a true picture but a document dating from the last few years of her life speaks of adventures and escapades which must have occurred before the visit to Egypt in 1873/4 which finally changed the course of her life and put an end to most of her travelling. This document was drafted as an autobiographical sketch in response to a request by the editor of an American periodical and it includes the following coolly off-hand passage:

> I have nearly broken my neck once or twice, but then I didn't break it - so possibilities go for nothing. I nearly shot one of my best friends once, while showing off a "Dorringer"; but then I didn't shoot her - so I was not tried for manslaughter. I was all but drowned one desperate midnight in Italy, when the horses, terrified by the rushing waters, and the glare of the torchlight around them, tried to back my travelling carriage off the ferry-boat in mid-stream when I was crossing the Po between Modena and Mantua - but if they had succeeded I should not now be writing...I was all but "backed", in like manner over a precipice in the Jura mountains, on another occasion. I have been in three earthquakes, and, as you know, have witnessed an eruption of Mount Vesuvius. Unfortunately, I was neither smashed, overwhelmed, nor swallowed up. Fate must have some dreadful destiny in store for me...

The ironic style of this is typical of her later manner when matters concerning herself and her feelings arise. It is reminiscent, for example, of the passage in *A Thousand Miles up the Nile* when she shrugs off a moment of unwonted panic with an ironic quip.

The eruption of Vesuvius referred to took place in 1872 and appears in *Lord Brackenbury*, the sole novel which Amelia published after going to

Egypt. She also gave an eyewitness account of it in the Village Hall, Westbury, on January 28th 1873, as a contribution to the "Penny Readings" series which were held there. As for the other adventures, they could have occurred at any time for, as her account of travelling in the Dolomites makes clear, she had no conventional timidities or squeamishness to deflect her from going where and as she wanted. Some may have dated from her wanderings in the 1850's and early '60's but others presumably fitted somehow into the pattern of her life at Westbury. An indication of at least one journey to Italy between 1860 and 1864 is to be found in her novel of 1865 called *Half a Million of Money*.

This novel is a positive brantub of stories, containing six or seven narrative lines squashed together. Some of the potential developments are aborted, others fizzle out in weak conclusions, the whole suggesting a narrative inventiveness exuberant to the point of incontinence. Among all the rest is the story of Giulio Colonna and his daughter Olimpia. Colonna is described as a man who has been "an enthusiast all his life", one who has

> for the last twenty or thirty years...devoted himself, heart and soul, to Italian politics. He has written more pamphlets and ripened more plots than any man in Europe. He is at the bottom of every Italian conspiracy. He is at the head of every secret society that has Italian unity for its object.

In other words, he is a modified Mazzini. Like Mazzini he is both idealistic and ruthless, demanding of his daughter, a patriot of the same stamp as himself, that she should sacrifice herself in a loveless marriage in order to secure the young man's millions for "the good cause". He tells her for good measure that he would give not only his own life but hers too without compunction if need were; but his ruthlessness is not allowed to issue in any disaster in the novel. The moral crux involving conflicting imperatives is not seriously faced and Colonna, fatally wounded in Italy, dies with his nobility as father and great leader essentially unstained. Meanwhile, the romantic young hero, Saxon, and his friend Lord Castletowers, have involved themselves in the Italian cause, landing with Colonna and even taking an active part in a battle. The account of Colonna's reception in Italy, the preliminaries of the battle, the topography, the battle itself, all are given with great vigour and in the most particular detail. At the very least, Amelia had studied accounts of the Italian struggles for liberation with an enthusiastic thoroughness which was characteristic of her and imagined its episodes with an intensity which always marks any scene or event which grips her powerfully. It would have been in her nature to travel to Italy and go over the ground herself and she may well have done so. That she had

21

been thrilled by the cause of Italian independence is beyond doubt and there are hints that it was Mazzini's (and Colonna's) republicanism which fired her more than the proclamation of the Kingdom of Italy in 1864. Saxon is Swiss and Switzerland comes in for much praise in the novel - the ideal republic perhaps?

The motto on the title page is "*O bella eta dell'oro*" (sic) which expresses well enough the joy of Italian liberation; but the gold of the motto has a literal as well as a metaphorical application. Lust for money is a theme throughout the book and the Colonnas share it with the others, albeit for motives which in their case are not directly self-seeking. Amelia was an afficianado of irony and no disdainer of puns. That this one carries a considerable ironic kick would make it specially appealing.

IV

Amelia is seen, then, at this point to be writing and travelling and responding energetically to the stimulus of events. Perhaps the pace slackened after 1864. Over the next six or seven years, at any rate, there came a change of mood. A letter of March 1871 marks the end of an era. The letter is addressed to a Mrs Cave, evidently a Westbury neighbour temporarily away from home. The tone is depressed. Amelia has been ill for three months, first with "a very dangerous throat attack (laryngitis)" and then, when she was beginning to recover from that, with "an attack of pressure on the brain." She has suffered from this twice before but the recent bout has been worse than anything earlier. It brought with it "a sort of half paralysis" and, since it was not brought on by over-work or "over-application of any kind", she found it particularly alarming. The laryngitis sounds like a recurrence of the trouble which led to cancellation of the singing engagment years before but "pressure on the brain" is more mysterious. Despite her rejection of the obvious explanation, continued exertion and the physical and mental demands she made upon herself seem the likely causes of the physical symptoms. Certainly her reaction to the impending departure from the district of two other friends, a Mr and Mrs Byrne, suggests an over-excited state of mind. "That great blow", she calls it, "the greatest that could befall me...It is like a death-blow to me". Mr Byrne was a clergyman, "a really good preacher with a really good accent", as Amelia described him in a letter to another member of the Cave family, but it seems that it was Mrs Byrne who was the more prominent in Amelia's life. Browning, who knew the household at The Larches, once sent a message to her in a letter but Marianne North, a close friend of Amelia's, took a less kindly view. Amelia was being bullied, she thought, and urged her "when the Byrne bullies you too much, come here".

The words Amelia uses about the imminent departure of the Byrnes recall those in which she describes the effect on her of her parents' death and they suggest a recurrence of desperate need for a mother-figure. In doing so they raise questions about Amelia's relations with Mrs Braysher at this time and the possibility that it was no longer providing the companionship and support Amelia looked for. An anecdote reported by Matilda Betham-Edwards may be pertinent. Amelia and Matilda met only infrequently in their adult life but there was enough sympathy between them for confidential conversation when they did. On one occasion, undated, they caught the attention of a wealthy woman who was in need of a companion. Amelia was already committed to Mrs Braysher so "Miss Brown" made her offer to Matilda. Amelia strongly advised her cousin not to allow herself to be caught by the bait of comfort and money although, as Matilda wryly notes, she had not taken her own advice. Hastily adjusting the impression she has given, that Amelia herself had been seduced by creature comforts, Matilda adds :

Adoption in her case was a matter of affection, by no means of personal interest. Having lost both her parents within a week of each other, she accepted the shelter of a friendly roof, retaining as much of independence as was possible under the circumstances.

The correction does not entirely obliterate the original suggestion and, as often with Matilda's testimony, the real significance of her remarks remains in several ways ambiguous. Does Amelia's advice to reject "Miss Brown" mean that she herself had come to regret her decision to accept "shelter" with Mrs Braysher? Had she found to her cost that independence was not easily preserved "under the circumstances"?

It would be unwise to make too much of Matilda's hints. She was herself a writer and to some extent the cousins got in each other's way. The common surname and the coincidence of the middle B., Betham or Blandford, led to constant confusion as the work of one was frequently ascribed to the other. Neither was prepared to sacrifice family pride by removing the B. though it would have been sensible for one of them to have done so. There was no real question of rivalry, for Matilda had a career of her own of which she was extremely proud, but some degree of equivocation lurks in her reminiscences of Amelia deriving, very probably, if not from jealousy then from a resentment hanging over from childhood when Amelia was the brilliant and the charming one for whom all rules were bent. Her report of the "Miss Brown" episode is significant all the same for its signal of difficulties that might arise in The Larches and the somewhat distraught tone of the 1871 letter may bespeak pressure not only "on the brain". It is to be noted that if the relationship with Mrs Braysher was sometimes stifling, Amelia's reaction was to turn to yet another substitute, Mrs Byrne: need, evidently, overweighed experience.

In 1871 the remedy for whatever was oppressing her was to go abroad and in the event the travels of the next two years were to be crucial. Through them she achieved the distinction she had sought from girlhood though not in a way that she could have anticipated. Hindsight, nevertheless, recognises in early years and early experiences the influences which stamped their character, for good or ill, on the achievements of her maturity.

II   The Dolomites and Egypt

Fleeing from Westbury in 1871, from ill-health, loss of friends and whatever else may have been weighing down on her, Amelia Edwards went first to Switzerland and then on to stay with friends in Florence. Winter was spent in Rome and in the spring she was in the south. June 1872 found her in the Italian lakes and there she decided to embark on what was virtually a pioneering expedition. Together with a friend she would explore "those mystic mountains beyond Verona which we know of, somewhat indefinitely, as the Dolomites." Out of this expedition came her first considerable travel book, published in 1873 under the title *A Midsummer Ramble in the Dolomites* and later as *Untrodden Peaks and Unfrequented Valleys*. It went through a number of editions in her lifetime and has been revived in several paperback editions since 1982.

This was not quite Amelia's first venture into travel writing for she had published as far back as 1862 a little book called *Sights and Stories: being some account of a holiday tour through the north of Belgium*; but this was tyro work, written while she was still picking up anything that would give her the means to live and reinforce her position as a professional writer. It is addressed to children and concerns a group of boys travelling with their master. There is a minimum of incident and the purpose is overtly pedagogic as the master imparts to his charges historical information and local legends appropriate to the various towns they visit. Amelia was toying at the time with the possibilities of writing for the juvenile market and contributed to "Every Boy's Magazine" and *Every Boy's Annual* as well as to an anthology of poems for children. Nothing suggests that talent was wasted when she abandoned the idea. *Untrodden Peaks*, on the other hand, is both entertaining and informative and in every respect a very accomplished piece of work. Whereas *Sights and Stories* struggles clumsily to accommodate narrative, instruction and humour, in *Untrodden Peaks* Amelia Edwards found the formula which was to serve her brilliantly in *A Thousand Miles up the Nile*. The creation of a narrative persona through whom everything can be mediated achieves both variety and cohesion and is the key to the success of both books. The extent to which personal history and character are reflected is a question always to be handled with care.

The Dolomites are now much admired and much frequented, a

popular playground for Italians and foreigners alike, but in Amelia's day this area of northern Italy bordering on Austria was untamed by roads and comfortable hotels and to most of her contemporaries it was *terra incognita*. "The general public is so slightly informed upon the subject", she wrote, "that it is by no means uncommon to find educated persons who have never heard of the Dolomites at all, or who take them for a religious sect, like the Mormons or the Druses." Her own imagination had been caught some fifteen years earlier when she had for the first time seen sketches of the mountains and been fascinated by their strange shape and colouring. Travel among them could only be on foot or on mule back, contact with the outside world could only be made with some difficulty and the amenities of conventional tourist travel were quite lacking. It could hardly be described as a "ramble" in any relaxed sense but to Amelia such considerations, far from being off-putting, were an attraction. What the better known great mountains and passes of the Alps had to offer seemed tame and unalluring by comparison; and, besides, by going off the beaten track, she would leave behind the tourists. There is an unusually waspish tone in Amelia's voice as she compares what she found in the Dolomites with what her experience would have been if she had joined the usual British flight from the Italian summer into Switzerland. The "arts of extortion" are unknown in the Dolomites, she tells her readers, "the old patriarchal notion of hospitality still survives, miraculously, in the minds of the inn-keepers" and "it is as natural to the natives of these hills and valleys to be kind, and helpful, and disinterested, as it is natural to the Swiss to be rapacious." She sums up: "here one escapes from hackneyed sights, from overcrowded hotels, from the dreary routine of tables d'hôtes, from the flood of Cook's tourists...life in the South-Eastern Tyrol is yet free from all the discomforts that have of late years made Switzerland unendurable". Evidently disillusion had set in since the panegyrics on Switzerland of *Half a Million of Money* seven years earlier.

With a woman friend - identified always only as L. - who shared her interests and her taste for adventure, she set off. With prudent forethought they shopped in Venice to provide against emergencies in case supplies should at any stage be unattainable - basics included two bottles of Cognac and four of Marsala - but the spice of the journey was the going into the unknown. They went as far as the railway could take them and then, using the present tense as she commonly does for special effect, Amelia confesses: "We have not the slightest idea of where we are going or of what we shall do when we get there".

They pursued, in fact, a twisting, convoluted route. Their principal object was to see as much of the mountains as they could but they were eager to take in as well whatever other sights of interest presented themselves on the way, be it a painting of an Italian master in a remote church or a rural wedding. Freedom to be the controllers of their journey, to follow their own whims, was one of its charms: they could linger, make diversions or accept the opportunity - embraced more enthusiastically by the intrepid and ever energetic Amelia than by L. - to make a first ascent of a mountain summit. Their appreciation of good, clean inns and friendly inn-keepers was sharpened by their willingness to accept if need be the bleak, the dirty and on one occasion, the plain horrific. They had ordered chicken for dinner: "Enough if I observe that the boiled chicken not only came to table in its headdress of feathers like an African chief *en grande tenue*, but also with its internal economy quite undisturbed."

Their independence and liberty to experience, for better or worse, the full range of adventure that the Dolomites could offer had not been attained without a struggle. L. had engaged a courier while in Naples before she joined Amelia and the courier was still in attendance in the north; but the courier's view of what it meant to be in the service of two English ladies received a painful shock when L. and Amelia, fortifying each other, abandoned their original plan of a tour in the Engadine and opted boldly for the Dolomites. The courier, whom Amelia treats with a mixture of derisive irony and mock-trepidation, was "a gentleman of refined and expensive tastes, who abhorred what is generally known by 'roughing it'". He despised primitive simplicity "and exacted that his employers should strictly limit their love of the picturesque to districts abundantly intersected by railways and well furnished with first class hotels." It was out of the question that "this illustrious man" should willingly accept the change of plan but at last he had to be told. Amelia, "never famous for moral courage" she says, ignominiously retreated but L. "undertook the service of danger", emerging from "that tremendous interview" composed but victorious; "and...the great man, greater than ever under defeat, comported himself thenceforth with such a nicely adjusted air of martyrdom and dignity as defies description."

Free from him, the women hired thenceforth mountain guides from the region, whose ways and characters they appreciated and who were no hindrance to their choice of route and company. There was easier contact with the natives of the mountains than there would later be with the Egyptians of mud villages on the Nile but though the contrast between the world they came from and that of the Egyptian fellahin was immeasurably greater, there was still an unbridgeable gap between the educated sophisticated women from middle England and the villagers of the Dolomites. Naturally enough, the class distinctions of the society she came from were implanted in Amelia's mind but she had no doubt that good manners were to be respected and reciprocated wherever they appeared.

"It is curious how soon one learns to be content with these humble Tyrolean albergos, and to regard as friends, and almost as equals, the kindly folks that keep them", she writes, and goes on to account for this by the fact that many of the Tyrolean innkeepers came from ancient families who in times past owned lands and filled responsible offices. She takes the opportunity to warn her fellow countrymen that they should behave to such people with due courtesy. "To treat them with hauteur, or with suspicion, or to give unneccessary trouble, is both unjust and impolitic." The ultimate result of such behaviour will be that the old inn-keeping families will close their doors against the English in disgust and "A class of extortionate speculators, probably Swiss, will step in and occupy the ground...and the simplicity, the poetry, the homely charm of the Dolomite district will be gone for ever." Clearly the Swiss had committed some grave offence.

The innkeepers and guides of the Dolomites were grateful to Amelia for her recommendations and for the publicity she gave to their region. They looked upon her, she reported, as their best friend and said she had been "the making" of them.

Her own behaviour was invariably friendly, gracious and polite but she never supposed or pretended to suppose a democratic equality between herself and the mountain people she met. That she respected and appreciated them stands to her credit but one episode uncovers a less attractive aspect of her dealings with the locals. L. and herself are desperately in need of side-saddles and only one is to be obtained. They obtain a loan of another for a while but when the time comes to relinquish it they succeed in bamboozling the young men charged with its return. They were "simple men with but few words at command" and no match for the smooth talking women who, with a mixture of lies and false promises, succeeded in persuading the reluctant young men to leave the saddle behind when they themselves went home. The young men knew, and Amelia knew, that they were likely to receive a very rough reception from their father when they returned empty handed. She is rueful but not repentant. The ladies' requirements are paramount even at the cost of some ruthlessness. Amelia and L. congratulate themselves on having successfully carried off their prize.

A more amusing illustration of English ladyhood occurs late in the journey when L. and Amelia encounter, in the yard of their inn and surrounded by a little group of boys and men, "a Phenomenon":

> It wears highlows [a kind of boot], a battered straw hat, and a brown garment which may be described either as a long kilt or the briefest of petticoats. Its hair is sandy; its complexion crimson; its age

anything between forty-five and sixty. It carries a knapsack on its back and an alpenstock in its hand. The voice is the voice of a man; the face, tanned and travel-stained as it is, is the face of a woman.

"It" is, in fact, female and she is " gabbling" German. Her story is evoking peals of laughter from her listeners. Their enquiry as to whether she had a guide in her travels is met with scorn:

> Not I! What do I want with a guide? ...Fatigue is nothing to me - distance is nothing to me - danger is nothing to me. I have been taken by brigands before now. What of that? If I had had a guide with me, would he have fought them? Not a bit of it! He would have run away. Well, I neither fought nor ran away. I made friends of my brigands - I painted their portraits - I spent a month with them; and we parted, the best comrades in the world.

This is caricature but it cuts two ways. It mocks the Phenomenon but it also reflects ironically on Amelia herself. The dismissal of the courier, the rough travel on the edge of steep drops, the primitive inns, the sketching of people encountered by the way - everything that Amelia and her companion have done is repeated in the Phenomenon's story but in far bolder colours and on far more dramatic lines. Was Amelia aware that her own adventures, requiring resource and determination and courage as undoubtedly they did, could hardly look other than pallid and cosy by comparison with those of a tough, swash-buckling character so far beyond convention that to call her unconventional would be too tame? Could she even in a mood of ironic self-awareness have invented the Phenomenon? Or did she mean the contrast between the uncouth foreigner and her own ladylike presence to show to her advantage? Her comment suggests the latter. "I don't know that I have ever experienced a more lively sense of gratification and relief," she writes, "than when I presently learn that this lady is German". Drawing her skirts about her, conscious of her gentility and the dignity of dress and manner which she always retains, she is deeply thankful that she does not have to recognise this grotesque travesty of the English lady traveller as a fellow-countrywoman. And yet - she did not have to add of the Phenomenon: "She paints, she botanises, [like Amelia and L.] and I think they said she writes". Amelia Edwards was a very intelligent woman, quite capable of recognising a parody of herself - or even of creating one - with all that it implied of difference and likeness. If thoughts of this kind entered her mind, she kept them off the paper, leaving only a hint, to be picked up or not. This is not by any means the only occasion in her writing when things unsaid seem to lie just out of sight, creating the slightest of ripples on the surface and teasing the reader with speculation about what it may be that lies submerged and unacknowledged.

Amelia was physically adventurous and at this time of her life appears to have been hardy in spite of earlier illnesses. She did not shrink from taking risks and seems never to have run short of vigour or enthusiasm. She was happy in the mountains for they satisfied many of her needs. They delighted her visual sense and she sketched them with loving accuracy. She developed at the same time her capacity for word-painting to delineate colour, contour, rock formation and every feature of craggy or pastoral landscape. Each detail is made vivid as the reader climbs with her or rides along a dizzying ledge or visits at more relaxed moments the mountain villages. In *Untrodden Peaks* as later in *A Thousand Miles* Amelia builds up animated scenes as though by a series of quick strokes of a painter's brush: the description of a motley crowd in Cortina at the beginning of Chapter Five is a case in point where her sharp and appreciative eye for colour is very evident. Drama, which she loved, is provided by the mountain scenery itself and encounters with local people give opportunities for miniature scenes of human life complete with dialogue. The deep satisfaction she took in precise fact is also catered for. With the same meticulous accuracy she would later apply to Egyptian archaeology she records the latest information gleaned from research about heights, climbing feats, routes and the flora of the mountains. Above all, in that beautiful and perilous environment she found what she seems always to have sought, something which would give a sharper edge to experience.

In her fiction melodrama and sensational event act as spurs to narrative and her predisposition to thrills of that kind is evident in *Untrodden Peaks*, as when she writes of her bedroom in one inn: "Tis as ghostly, echoing, suicidal a place to sleep in as ever I saw in my life!" Like the young Wordsworth, she is startled one day by the sudden looming presence of a mountain hitherto invisible and the shock arouses in her, as in him, a sense of "unknown modes of being"; but Amelia Edwards lays no claim to mystical intimation. She sees instead "A great blue wrinkled glacier, reaching down out of the mist like a terrible Hand", an idea to be relished and stored up, perhaps, for a tale sometime.

In life also she looked for what would heighten and stimulate. When the descent from the mountains had at last to be made, "Here is the hot, dusty, busy, dead-level World of the Commonplace again!" she exclaims as she and L. re-enter once more "normal" life. They are significant words. Throughout her life Amelia took challenging options for the sake of the demands and the stimulus involved, whether physical, as in the mountains, or intellectual, as when she determined to win herself a place as a journalist and novelist and later to make herself an Egyptologist. In her later life she

30

worked excessively, another manifestation of her urge to squeeze the most out of whatever experience was open to her: mountain climbing no longer being feasible, she gave herself extravagantly to a cause. As the courier in the Dolomites discovered, it was not in her nature to settle for the expected life of a woman of her time and class with all the restrictions which polite, and especially English, society demanded. To go abroad, and when there to get off the beaten track or go beyond the usual tourist interests, was a resource which gave free play to her energies and her talents and which produced *Untrodden Peaks* and, a few years later, the most complete and successful expression of all she had to offer, *A Thousand Miles up the Nile*.

In her personal attachments Amelia veered between the need for domestic security on the one hand and, on the other, for a companion who shared sufficient common ground to be willing to accompany her in travel and allow her free rein to explore and adventure as she wished. L. was one such companion and the partnership was evidently successful for it was renewed when she accompanied Amelia also to Egypt. As an important figure in Amelia's life, at least in this period, she and the nature of the relationship between the two women deserve some attention.

The friend who accompanied Amelia in the Dolomites and afterwards in Egypt, designated in the books only by the initial L., was a Miss Lucy Renshawe. In the absence of other information, her character and role in Amelia's life at this time have to be pieced together as well as may be from such small clues as there are here and there in the texts. She was smaller than Amelia, or at any rate not so sturdy, since a smaller horse was assigned to her in the Dolomites. She was not so enthusiastic as Amelia at accepting the challenge of a first ascent of the Sasso Bianco but if she lacked something of Amelia's physical energy and interpidity, she was on occasions bolder than her friend. It was she who tackled the haughty courier and broke the news that they were abandoning the well-trodden and comfortably provisioned tourist tracks and were to strike out into the unknown and undomesticated mountains. Amelia, less valiant in confrontation, shirked the task and it was L. who finally dismissed him. The courier to some extent forestalled her by tendering his resignation when the full enormity of his employers' plans became clear to him, but his offer of a fortnight's notice was rejected and "he was then and there paid off and done with", the affair being conducted by L. "with an amount of withering sang froid that speedily reduced the offender to a condition of abject humility."

L., in fact, was responsible for the presence of this lordly character in the first place since she had hired him in Naples before Amelia joined her. L. also had with her, both in Italy and in Egypt, a maid, facts which suggest that she was at least a fairly wealthy woman and one whom the courier believed could support him in the style to which he was accustomed. She appears not to have been over-tender about her employees. Whatever the courier may have deserved, the maid is a rather pathetic figure, abandoned for days at a time in a strange country whose language she does not speak while her mistress and friend go off on excursions with their guides. No wonder she looks "mournful" (Amelia's word). Perhaps even this was better than riding (she had not ridden before) on a crudely improvised saddle - for there was no third decent one to be obtained, even by the felonious means employed by Amelia and L. to provide for themselves. But L., true to English tradition, could be sentimental about animals and, "though unused to the melting mood" as Amelia comments, took a sentimental farewell of her mule.

L. has a marked presence in *Untrodden Peaks*, less so in *A Thousand Miles up the Nile*. Julia Keay in her book, *With Passport and Parasol*, ignores *Untrodden Peaks* and paints a pathetic picture of L. in Egypt as a down-trodden woman always over-ridden by a dominating and bullying Amelia. This is quite beside the mark. Other considerations aside, it is clear from *Untrodden Peaks* that L. was perfectly well able to stand up for herself and that there was no question of Amelia browbeating her. The misunderstanding arises from the fact that Amelia is misplaced among the group of women brought together in *With Passport and Parasol*. Their travels were impelled by quite different motives from hers and evoked quite different qualities of character. The misfit results in an unsympathetic treatment amounting to serious misrepresentation, distortion of the relations between Amelia and L. being one example of this.

Julia Keay's mistaken picture can be dismissed but what precisely the true nature of the relationship was is not so easily decided. That they were lesbian lovers is a possibility to which an episode in *Untrodden Peaks* may lend some colour. Amelia and L. have arrived at a small roadside inn and they and their belongings become the objects of immense curiosity to the four women who live there. One of them takes it upon herself to question the strangers - where do they come from? how have they travelled? and, finally, have they travelled alone? "Poor little things! poor little things!" she exclaims as they answer. "Are you sisters?" "Are you married?":

Another negative, whereat her surprise amounts almost to consternation. 'Come! Not married? Neither of you?' 'Neither of us', I reply, laughing. 'Gran' dio! Alone and not married! Poverine! poverine!' Hereupon they all cry 'poverine' in chorus, with an air of such genuine concern and compassion that we are almost ashamed of the irrepressible laughter with which we cannot help receiving their condolences.

Collision between the sophisticated and the naive may certainly raise laughter: the question here is, what is at the root of the sophistication? Is it implied that Amelia and L. experience a marriage which not only has no need of a man but is so far superior that they cannot but laugh at the idea that they are to be pitied? Or does it simply underline the difference in background and experience of the educated English ladies and the inn women: "mere savages - rosy, hearty, good-natured: but as ignorant and uncivilised as aboriginal Australians". Amelia and L., independent of means and of character, happy in their power to travel as and when they liked, could well be amused at the simple women's compassion for their state. The second interpretation is at least as plausible as the first but the episode remains ambiguous. After all, the inn women, ignorant as they might be, were only saying what society back home would say and Amelia herself, in an earlier episode, having persuaded a beautiful peasant woman to sit for her portrait, asks her if she is married:

No, Signora
Nor betrothed?
No, Signora
But that must be your own fault, I said.

Amelia's questions and her response to the answers are those of any conventional woman of her day and the same in essence as those of the peasant women to her and L. Social difference is no doubt largely responsible for the discrepant attitudes which are assumed towards the two episodes. Marriage, Amelia might argue, would seem a natural career for the beautiful farm servant who at twenty-three had an air of "impenetrable melancholy" but for herself and L. there were other opportunities and they needed no husband to support them. Some insecurity is betrayed nevertheless, by rather too insistent laughter and a spontaneous question to a farm girl.

The nature of Amelia's attachments to other women is not susceptible of easy labelling. The evidence of her early life, the thwarted attachment to the Irish cousin, her male friendships in France, the unmistakable sexuality of the portrait of Hamel, all suggest a heterosexual orientation; but when she reviewed the male bodies in the Paris baths and found them "all more or less hideous", it may not have been only her artistic sensibilities which were offended. The death of her mother threw into prominence a very strong need for female support and she turned first to Mrs Braysher and then for a time became reliant more than Marianne North thought reasonable on Mrs Byrne. It is Amelia's friendship with

Marianne North herself, however, which brings the possibility of lesbianism most insistently to the fore.

Marianne North (1830-90) came from a more secure and better provided social background than Amelia but like her she was deeply devoted to one parent - in her case her father - and formed no other attachment which was comparable in depth of feeling. When he died in 1869 she chose to follow an independent life and set out on remarkable journeys which took her over some dozen years to every continent of the world. Her object was to make a pictorial record of tropical and exotic plants and the outcome was a collection of more than eight hundred paintings. They are now housed in the gallery which she built at Kew and which is named after her. She was for some years closely in touch with Amelia Edwards and wrote her long letters from her various destinations, detailing her movements and her findings. By mutual agreement, Amelia used material from them in articles which kept the public in touch with her progress and adventures.

The two women had much in common. Both had studied music and Marianne North had in early years, like Amelia, a beautiful singing voice but music yielded the primacy to art in the affections of them both. Marianne's writing reveals a lively and observant personality and a sense of humour that could be satirical: the temperamental match would seem to be very close.

The letters which Marianne North wrote while still in England and preparing for her travels are the most interesting from the point of view of the relationship between the two. There were many of these letters. Judging by those of Marianne North that survive and are kept in Somerville College, Oxford, their correspondence must have gone near to equalling the record of daily or twice daily missives despatched to each other by those famous lovers, the Brownings. Amelia's own letters do not appear to have survived but Marianne's replies give the tone of them, "those wonderful long letters of love" she calls them. Her own letters are affectionate, brisk, cheerful and not at all introspective. They can hardly be described as love letters though Marianne is not entirely unresponsive to "dearest Amelia's" demonstrativeness. She accepts it - but always with qualifications. "Nice to have your petting at the last moment", she writes "- for I do like it - rather - though what should put it into your head to do it I can't think!" Amelia wants to buy her a gold ring to take with her in her absence but Marianne is evidently wary of the symbolism: "If you really do require to tie me up in that way give me a silver one...I shall not forget you in a hurry though I can't write sentiments." The impression given by these letters is of a kindly and well-disposed Marianne trying to cool down an emotionally over-wrought Amelia: "Bless you! what love letters you do write, what a pity you waste them on a woman!" She could hardly signal more clearly that as far as she is concerned a more fervent relationship is not in question. It seems typical that Amelia kept Marianne's letters but Marianne does not appear to have kept Amelia's.

That Amelia had lesbian inclinations at this stage in her life may be true but how much significance to attach to this is doubtful. At some early stage she determined to pursue an independent career, a decision which could have followed disappointment or frustration in love or might have been a deliberate refusal to take on the subordinate and restricted role of wife in contemporary marriage. She cherished her freedom and her independence and she was certainly keenly aware of the crippling disadvantages which marriage imposed on a woman. In a lecture of later years she spoke scornfully of what she called "one of the pleasant fictions of our marriage service" whereby a man promises to endow his wife with all his worldly goods. "We know that nothing is in reality farther from his intentions", she comments, the reality being that it is only after years of agitation that the bride's rights to even her own property have been secured.

The role of her mother in her life was certainly a powerful one and the extent of its repercussions wide. That her death sent Amelia looking for a replacement makes clear her need for the support of another woman, even though like Mrs Byrne she may have "bullied" her. For years, home with Mrs Braysher and travel with L. may have satisfied her but in 1869, when Marianne North began to contemplate her world-wide expeditions, Amelia Edwards was approaching forty. Over the next two years she became very ill, a prey to severe though undetermined pressures. The special stress of this period may well have owed something to years of sexual abstinence or frustration and if she became passionately heated in her feeling for Marianne, her emotions enflamed further by the prospect of long periods of absence, it would not be surprising. Diagnosis in all the circumstances must needs be cautious. In any event she seems to have been able to relax the tension, finding relief and pleasure as usual in a strenuous programme of travel and regaining an equilibrium which appears never again to have been disturbed in the same way.

In just over twelve months Amelia was in Switzerland, Florence, Rome, and Naples, and then exploring the Dolomites. The descent from the mountains to the "dead-level World of Commonplace" at the end of the Dolomite expedition was unwelcome and in the summer of 1873 she was off again, still with L., on a walking tour of France. Their intentions this time, however, were to be stymied by an opposition which could not be faced down: the weather. It rained, and it went on raining and even Amelia and L. were forced in the end to surrender. Desperately seeking sunshine and warmth they did not much mind where they found them. They considered Algiers, Malta and Cairo and having decided on Cairo they set off even more casually than they had embarked on their Dolomite excursion: "The thing was no sooner decided than we were gone...without definite plans, outfit, or any kind of Oriental experience". They intended, of course, to go up the Nile but beyond that all was vague. It was, as it turned out, a momentous decision though it was far from seeming so at the time. The book which resulted is the peak of Amelia's career as a writer as it is also her best-known contribution to the new science of egyptology: it marks the climax of one career and the opening of another.

II

Going to Egypt to-day is a matter only of a few hours' flight but in the nineteenth century it was an expedition requiring time, stamina and grit. In 1846 Harriet Martineau started out from Marseilles in a ship swarming with cockroaches, insufficiently supplied with coal and at the mercy of a captain who, happy enough to pass his time with a flirtatious widow, was cheerfully unconcerned as days and weeks passed, food ran out and the end of the journey grew no nearer. Eventually a steamer came out from Malta in search of the ship which was so behind time that it was reported to have gone to the bottom. This was more than usually horrendous but not altogether exceptional and conditions did not improve strikingly over the next thirty years. Amelia Edwards's journey from Brindisi to Alexandria in 1873 was storm-tossed and otherwise uncomfortable and at the end of it forty-eight hours of quarantine had to be endured. Such travellers' tales were only too familiar and in *A Thousand Miles up the Nile* she draws a veil over the process of arrival and instead presents her first morning in Cairo as though it had been a magic translation from one country to another. She wakes, she says, at sun-rise, to see palm trees waving in a rose-coloured dawn and "a veiled lady walking on [a] terraced roof in the midst of a cloud of pigeons...Nothing could be more simple than the scene and its accessories; nothing, at the same time, more Eastern, strange and unreal".

Amelia's dramatic instincts are much to the fore in the opening pages of *A Thousand Miles up the Nile*. She introduces first the scene in the dining-room of Shepheard's Hotel, Cairo, with its cosmopolitan collection of Anglo-Indians, European residents, winter visitors and Nile-goers. The entry of two strange women, herself and L., sun-burnt and travel-stained, rouses the immediate curiosity of the diners. The *mise-en-scène* would fit a mystery-story well but for the touch of light irony which becomes fully apparent when she describes how she and L. came to be there:

...in simple truth we had drifted hither by accident, with no excuse of health or business, or any serious object whatever; and had just taken refuge in Egypt as one might turn aside into the Burlington Arcade or the Passage des Panoramas - to get out of the rain.

The visit soon acquired a mission, however, for Longman, Amelia's publisher, no sooner heard where she was than he commissioned a book. He might do so with confidence since *Untrodden Peaks* had shown unequivocally how successfully she could handle this kind of assignment.

The Dolomites were virtually unknown when Amelia undertook her "ramble" but Egypt by 1873 was already thoroughly opened-up tourist territory and Amelia and L. plunge into social life in Cairo with a will. They make the most of the spectacles on offer such as the Cairo bazaars, a performance of whirling dervishes and the departure of a caravan for Mecca. The vivacity of description and the evidence which these opening pages give of the gift of bringing a scene to life are a foretaste of the pleasures to come in *A Thousand Miles up the Nile*. Nile travel involved more than this, of course, and to combine the anecdotal with the archaeological posed a challenge requiring both skill and tact. Here *Untrodden Peaks* had already given Amelia some practice for her interest in mountains was a serious one and in her book she spares no pains in providing information as full and precise as she can make it. When she comes to write *A Thousand Miles* she applies again the technique developed in the earlier book, of using a persona through whom she can modulate from the light-hearted to the scholarly and control the mood and tempo at every stage. Having determined from the start to take seriously the archaeological aspects of the Nile journey she introduces her readers to them gently, taking pains to reassure them by presenting herself as a friendly and humorous personality who, however well informed she may turn out to be, will never be pretentious or over-bearing.

The main business of the time spent in Cairo was to hire a dahabeeyah. Shallow and flat-bottomed, these boats were adapted for either sailing or rowing and were comfortably appointed for the foreigners who lived on them for weeks or months at a time. Amelia Edwards and L. hired one of the biggest, measuring a hundred feet from stem to stern and twenty feet across the upper deck at its broadest. For crew and attendants, they engaged a captain, a steersman and twelve sailors, plus a dragoman (interpreter), head cook, assistant cook, two waiters and the boy who cooked for the crew. Amelia and L. had the boat to themselves when they set out from Cairo but they planned to pick up four other travellers at a point further south. One of these, Andrew McCallum, was a painter and already known to Amelia. *In A Thousand Miles up the Nile* she refers to him throughout, anonymously, as "the Painter". McCallum was an experienced Nile traveller and his intention was to paint a big picture at Abu Simbel. The others were friends of his, not previously known to Amelia, a Mr and Mrs Ayr who were accompanied by their maid. They had been married less than a month and Amelia introduces them with a characteristic blend of irony and provocative reticence: "Of people who are struggling through that helpless phase of human life called the honeymoon, it is not fair to say more than that they are both young enough to make the situation interesting." They also are not named in the book but dubbed "the Idle Man" - he has scholarship, delicate health and leisure - and she, with no distinguishing feature, is called "the Little Lady". When the party was complete there were twenty-five on board.

Amelia and L., taking possession of the boat at Cairo, were no sooner embarked than they set about making their surroundings "cosy and home-like". "It is wonderful," Amelia writes, " what a few books and roses, an open piano, and a sketch or two will do." That first afternoon they sat on the upper deck, furnished as it was with lounge-chairs, tables and rugs "like a drawing-room in the open air", and prepared to settle down to get to know their crew and study the strange land through which they were travelling.

The first experience was idyllic but life on the Nile was far from being a sunny passage through continuously delightful landscapes any more than the *Philae*, good example of its class as it was, could offer the comforts and security of a modern Nile steamer. The journey took many weeks and the sun did not always shine or sometimes shone too hot. There were strong head winds against which progress could only be made by muscle power as the men pulled the boat along by ropes like cart-horses. Sometimes not even that was possible and there was nothing for it but to moor and, rocking and buffeted as the boat was blown against the shore, wait for calmer times. There were sand storms which also made progress impossible and in addition filled eyes, mouth, hair and ears, clothes and everything else with sand. At times of low water there were sand banks on which a vessel might run and be marooned or even split, as had happened to a Cook's steamer which Amelia's party saw. Its passengers had managed to get ashore and had spent the night in tents, waiting to be rescued piece-meal as other boats came up and took off as many as they could accommodate. Amelia and her party experienced a hurricane which lasted for thirty-six hours. There were also cataracts to be negotiated, thrilling but dangerous moments when a miscalculation by the pilot would bring a boat irreparably to grief. Natives on the whole were friendly though importunate calls for baksheesh and the attentions of would-be traders could be (then as now) a harrassment. At Beni Suef, a town with a bad reputation, it was considered desirable when the *Philae* moored there to post guards at night but the guards slept all through the only minor disturbance there was and no harm was done. Nevertheless, an escort of sailors was always taken on shore.

Most trying of all must have been the delays. It was wonderful, if one had like Amelia the taste for it, to be able to spend days or weeks exploring a site (fourteen days in Abu Simbel, for instance) studying it in every detail and getting to know it intimately - intimacy, in fact, was unavoidable if one was to see anything at all for there was none of the lighting, the walkways, the carefully prepared arrangements for easy viewing which pamper the Nile traveller of to-day. It might be necessary to crawl into a tomb or slide down into the darkness on one's stomach. Inside there might well be bats and the only illumination was by flares held by Arab attendants or a bunch of candles tied to the end of a stick. If any benefit was to be derived at all it had to be by minute scrutiny and by some exertion. To those with any interest in what they were seeing the time and the effort were well worth it but the lengthy and recurrent periods of enforced idleness when the wind did not blow or blew in the wrong direction and there was nothing to be done and little to see were a trial to all but the most dedicated.

In fair conditions, however, it was a far from lonely life. Nile travel was a fashionable thing in the 1870's. The Prince and Princess of Wales had gone up in 1862 and the Empress Eugenie followed suit in 1869. (In Cairo, incidentally, she caused panic in the breasts of officials when she composedly sat herself down to rest in a chair last claimed by Queen Hatshepsut some three thousand years before: whether their care was more for the Empress or the chair, who can say?). When Amelia was there the river was alive with fellow-English, Americans (the next most numerous), Germans, Belgians and French. A Miss Marianne Brocklehurst and her companion, Miss Booth, had sailed on the same boat from Brindisi with Amelia and L. and they took a dahabeeyah up the Nile at the same time. The friendship which developed offered welcome companionship and also a spice of friendly though fierce rivalry at times when there was competition to be first at a mooring and secure the best position. The ladies of each boat bargained heartily for antiques and Miss Brocklehurst eventually amassed a collection which is housed in the Macclesfield Museum in Manchester, itself built and endowed by her.

Miss Brocklehurst kept a diary and a comparison of that with *A Thousand Miles* provides a piquant contrast in attitudes. Miss Brocklehurst was an intelligent woman and she was conscientious in visiting all the important sites, at least briefly. Some of them impressed her greatly but she was not drawn to make a serious study. She thought well of Kom Ombo but of its history she remembers only that it was "built by a Ptolemy somebody and finished by a somebody Caesar". At Edfu she remarks that "The pylons are immense but we do not like pylons". This insouciant attitude would have struck a chord with many, perhaps most, Nile travellers who would probably also have agreed with her complaints about the weather and the dirt and dishonesty of Arabs. It is all very different from *A Thousand Miles up the Nile*. Amelia's record is not a false one but it is animated first by her own unstinting enthusiasm and, second, by the wish to send visitors to Egypt with eyes and minds open to sights and ideas beyond their usual ken. Discomforts are allowed to count for very little when in her estimation the positive gains are so overwhelmingly great.

More transitory friendships might be struck up with a number of boats and at Luxor there was "a round of gaiety". A "joyous party" would gather for picnic lunch among the ruins of great temples: Edward Lear gives an account of one such on the island of Philae when he feasted on macaroni, turkey, rock pigeons and pancakes. Amelia's account of a lunch party in the Ramasseum becomes a full-scale picture of oriental exotica: the great columns, the Persian rugs spread on the ground "the dragoman in his picturesque dress going to and fro - the brown and tattered arabs, squatting a little way off, silent and hungry - each with his string of forged scarabs, his imitation gods, or his bits of mummy-case and painted cartonnage for sale - the glowing peeps of landscape framed in here and there through vistas of columns - the emblazoned architraves laid along from capital to capital overhead, each block sculptured with enormous cartouches yet brilliant with vermilion and ultramarine - the patient donkeys munching all together at a little heap of vetches in one corner - the intense depths of cloudless blue above." The ability to produce, as here, the verbal equivalent of a David Roberts or a Werner is one of the repertoire of skills which Amelia Edwards draws upon in *A Thousand Miles* but she has discretion enough not to overplay it.

One reason for restraint was her recognition that there was more to eastern life than the material for romantic pictures. "An artist might pass a winter there", she writes, "and not exhaust the pictorial wealth of those five miles which divide Assuan from Philae" and she goes on to describe it in brilliant painterly style. Then she adds:

It is all so picturesque, indeed so biblical, so poetical, that one is almost in danger of forgetting that the places are something more than beautiful backgrounds, and that the people are not merely appropriate figures placed there for the delight of sketchers, but are made of living flesh and blood, and moved by hopes and fears, and sorrows, like our own.

Among Amelia's qualities is her willingness to backtrack: she makes an instinctive, perhaps conventional, approach but then her intelligence catches up and corrects it. In her attitude to the native Egyptians, however, there is a tension which is never resolved: she feels for them but she does not feel with them as one striking episode makes clear. One of her companions, shooting at quail, hits a baby and provokes, naturally enough one might think, the anger of local people. The self-righteous behaviour of the Europeans in this crisis, even before it is found that the baby is only slightly grazed, is at the least unattractive but Amelia will go no further in comment than gentle mockery of "the Idle Man" who did the shooting and an expression of shame at the gross disproportion of the punishment pronounced by the local Egyptian authority for the burst of native anger: she is careful to record that her companions intercede to prevent more than a token punishment being carried out.

British and Arab assumptions and historical backgrounds clash in this episode without possibility of real understanding between them. There is some discomfort for the modern reader in Amelia's treatment of it as perhaps there was for her too. It reflects, in fact, a recurrent problem, one faced no doubt by many sensitive travellers then and later and exacerbated for Amelia Edwards by her disposition to seize with quasi-professional enthusiam on the pictorially rich and the dramatic without necessarily thinking of the human situations involved. She has been told that there are fine subjects for painting in a slave market and, to the great chagrin of the Governor of Assuan who strongly denies that there is slave-trading in Egypt, she enquires eagerly as to how she may get to see one. Excitement at the prospect of great material for sketching overwhelms those "English notions" which she has earlier said were shocked when she and L. first saw the sailors tracking: "it looked like slaves' work"; but, as she also said "we got used to it, as one gets used to everything in time". A troubled mind may comfort itself with the thought that perhaps, after all, the feelings of Egyptian fellahin or slaves, are not "like ours"; and in any case, it is not for foreigners to interfere. The forced labour of the corvée may be harsh, slavery an abomination, the harem system condemn women to empty lives, the condition of the children of the very poor too distressing to be bearable - "One would willingly go any number of miles out of the way rather than witness their suffering, without the power to alleviate it" - but what can a foreigner do but pass by, feed mind and eyes, tell the story on return and meanwhile enjoy what is there to be enjoyed, however uneasily at times? So Amelia oscillates between sympathy, even fellow-feeling, and alienation; not an uncommon experience at any time and honestly exposed by her.

The cultural problems which underlie all travel, more acutely in some areas than others, surface by implication rather than statement in *A Thousand Miles* but where individual grief is concerned Amelia's responsiveness is unconstrained. It may relate to the strength of her own relationship with her mother that two notable passages where another's pain is sharply felt concern grieving mothers. Amelia and friends witness the desert funeral of a young man and Amelia takes note particularly of the grief of "the desolate mother". On another occasion an old woman comes to the boat to ask if the sailors have any news of her son, Yusef, who has gone to Cairo and from whom she has not heard for nearly a year:

> It made one's heart ache to see the tremulous eagerness with which the poor soul put her questions, and the crushed look in her face when she turned away.

More often, however, Amelia's tone is light as she observes the scene around her. Her sense of humour and her sharp eye for a simile vivify scenes and events of all kinds. "A select society of vultures perched all in a row upon a ledge of rock" are "solemn as the bench of bishops" (a wicked comparison!); traders in a country bazaar sit cross-legged in their cupboard-like shops "like shabby old idols in shabby old shrines"; five sailors sitting cross-legged on a mud divan have had their heads newly lathered by the Luxor barber who is surveying his work "much as an artistic cook might survey a dish of particularly successful *meringues à la crême*. The meringues looked very sheepish as we laughed and passed by".

The book is full of such touches and, on a larger scale, the Painter's encounter with the Sheykh of the Cataract becomes a joyous piece of comic narrative. The Painter, an old Nile hand, has compiled "a little vocabulary of choice Arabic maledictions" as a resource in case of need. His companions treat his lexicon as a joke but when on their way up river the Sheykh of the Cataract appears to be dragging out time and running up expense unnecessarily, the Painter in exasperation takes out his book of curses and delivers a choice extract from his garnered store:

> The Sheykh sprang to his feet as if he had been shot - turned pale with rage under his black skin - vowed the *Philae* might stay where she was till doomsday, for aught that he or his men would do to help her a foot farther - bounded into his own ricketty sandal and rowed away, leaving us to our fate.

On the boat all were aghast. What was to be done? Of the alternatives, "The majority were for immolating the Painter"; but next morning, lo and behold, there arrived the Sheykh of the Cataract, all smiles and all activity - "We were his dearest friends now. The Painter was his brother". The cataract Nubians worked that day as they had never worked before. From thenceforth the Painter's book was safe from all derision:

> If that note-book of his had been the drowned book of Prospero, or the magical Papyrus of Thoth fished up anew from the bottom of the Nile, we could not have regarded it with a respect more nearly bordering upon awe.

Human comedy is the essence of that episode. The collision of human and human, though, is as nothing to the collision of human and camel:

> You know that he hates you, from the moment you first walk round him, wondering where and how to begin the ascent of his hump. He does not, in fact, hesitate to tell you so in the roundest terms. He swears freely while you are taking your seat; snarls if you but move in the saddle; and stares you angrily in the face, if you attempt to turn his head in any direction save that which he himself prefers. Should you persevere, he tries to bite your feet. If biting your feet does not answer, he lies down.

This is worse, for "the lying down and getting-up of a camel are performances designed for the express purpose of inflicting grievous bodily harm upon his rider". When in motion he has an agenda of four paces:

> A short walk, like the rolling of a small boat in a chopping sea; a long walk that dislocates every bone in your body; a trot that reduces you to imbecility; and a gallop that is sudden death. One tries in vain to imagine a crime for which the *peine forte et dure* of sixteen hours on camel-back would not be a full and sufficient expiation. It is a punishment to which one would not willingly be the means of condemning any human being - not even a reviewer.

The entrance of the reviewer comes as a shock, so direct a reference to her personal life being a rarity indeed for Amelia Edwards.

In contrast to this account of the camel and his irreducible bloody-mindedness is her meditation on that humble but highly regarded insect, the Egyptian beetle or scarab. The two passages together illustrate something of the range of styles and moods which Amelia has at her command to give life and variety to *A Thousand Miles*. The camel is excoriated, feelingly and comically, but the beetle is both pitied and honoured. Amelia writes of observing one particular specimen which was

> busily engaged in the preparation of a large rissole of mud, which he presently began laboriously propelling up the bank...His rissole was at least four times bigger than himself, and to pull it up that steep incline to a point beyond the level of next summer's inundation was a labour of Hercules for so small a creature.

The "rissole" contained eggs and the beetle's task was to roll it to a place on the edge of the desert and bury it in the sand where it would be safe from the rising water. Having provided for his successors the beetle dies content (presumably). The ancient peoples of Egypt observed the heroic endeavours of their beetle and with their myth-making imagination invested him with a symbolism which finally conferred upon him a special sacredness. For them he became an emblem of divine creative and preserving power and even of the immortality of the soul. "One sees how subtle a lesson", Amelia comments, "the old Egyptian moralists had presented to them for contemplation, and with how fine a combination of wisdom and poetry they regarded this little black scarab..." Then with a touch of ironic amusement, she adds,

> As a type, no insect has ever had so much greatness thrust upon him. He became a hieroglyph, and stood for a word signifying both To Be and To Transform. His portrait was multiplied a million-fold...

The scarab successfully bore the load that Ancient Egyptian moralists placed upon him but he could well have been robbed of his mystique by a nineteenth century sentimentalist. Amelia's touch is far too sure and her mind too sharp for that. The single word "rissole", just as it deflates spurious dignity, so also it sets Amelia's signature on the passage. Sympathy allied to an instinct to stand back and note with amusement the incongruous and the absurd is a mark of many passages in *A Thousand Miles* and is shown again here as the tone modulates skilfully from rissoles to meditation and from that to the irrepressible smile with which Shakespeare and the scarab are made acquainted with each other.

The dig at reviewers which concludes her robust deglamourising of the camel, sometimes so romantically called "the ship of the desert", comes as a surprise in the context but it is appropriate enough that at some point Amelia should remind her readers of her previous career as a novelist. Egypt engaged her intellect and her emotions more fully and more deeply than any subject had done before and it stirred her to the fullest

44

development of her powers but these powers were not new endowments. She had been serving her apprenticeship for the writing of *A Thousand Miles* ever since she first determined that literature would be her career. Some years later she would be praised for the writing she did to publicise and rouse interest in the work of the Egypt Exploration Society and she replied that it was not surprising that she was able to catch the public's imagination more successfully than the archaeologists could do in their reports. None of them, she points out, had worked as she had to master the art of engaging the reader nor studied like her the subtleties of language. From the moment she decided on writing as her career she had, in her own words, "cultivated style - worked at it as if it were a science - and mastered it. I study style", she goes on, "like a poet, calculating even the play of vowel sounds and the music of periods. Style is an instrument which I have practised sedulously, and which I can play upon". The ease and the charm of *A Thousand Miles* fully bear out her words. The musical career which had failed her in earlier life now comes into its own, as her choice of words in the quotation above acknowledges. Similarly, her ambition to be an artist, painfully frustrated when she was young, now makes its positive contribution and gives her the eye for detailed, accurate and vivid scene painting; her sense of reader-reaction bred by years of journalism and the writing of fiction enables her to understand the need for constantly renewed stimulus to mind and imagination. *A Thousand Miles up the Nile* was an immediate success and more than a hundred years later continues to entertain and instruct a later generation of readers, very different in many ways though they be and although Egypt itself, unchanging for thousands of years, has been moved at last by the forces of the modern world.

The anecdotal, personal, travelogue aspects of *A Thousand Miles* count for much but there is more, for the book carries a freight of serious research and thought. That, face to face with the monuments of Ancient Egypt, Amelia Edwards would wish to learn as much about them as she possibly could and that she would not be content with vague knowledge or a misty impression is evident from everything that she had ever undertaken. She had, like John Donne back in the seventeenth century, "an immoderate, hydroptic thirst" for learning and she had, besides, a compelling urge to share with others the refreshment she found in knowledge. *Untrodden Peaks* is replete with facts to enhance, Amelia hopes, the appreciation of the arm-chair climber and to give practical assistance to any who may follow in her footsteps or go further. Her novels are stuffed full of information on virtually every subject within the Victorian intellectual sphere. Plot and characterisation are not strong enough to absorb this intellectual matter comfortably but in *Untrodden Peaks* the problem of form is solved by the framework of a journey and, even more importantly, by the creation of an author persona, amused and amusing, alert and observant, well-informed but not pedantic, who holds all the strands together with grace and ease of manner. The same recipe works even better *In A Thousand Miles up the Nile* : Amelia Edwards invented herself as author-persona more successfully than she invented any of her fictional characters.

As McCallum and "the happy couple" have been given their labels, so Amelia refers to herself in *A Thousand Miles* as the Writer. She wants to identify herself as the narrator and to make clear her professional equality with the Painter, neither of whom is to be in any way confounded with a dilettante like the Idle Man: it is noticeable that she speaks always of "work" as she studies and records what she finds on the journey. The title also saves her from ubiquitous use of the egotistical "I" and it allows her to preserve a distance between herself and her persona. The Writer is not identical with Amelia Edwards though she comes of the same stock; she is the product of selection, a carefully controlled image which steps well short of soul-baring. She was personally among the most reserved of writers but she achieved her greatest triumph by a projection of her own character deliberately fashioned for public acceptance.

Writer she was and not explorer. Intrepid and indefatigable by most standards, her exploits pale by comparison with those of Julia Keay's heroines or of the naturalist, Mary Kingsley, who paddled her canoe through mangrove swamps and was once saved from impalement in a game-pit by the voluminous Victorian skirt she insisted on wearing in all circumstances. Amelia Edwards's distinction lies in her gifts as a writer which, very successfully deployed in *Untrodden Peaks*, were even more brilliantly expressed in *A Thousand Miles* ; but the journey to Egypt turned her into an Egyptologist and ever after it is as an Egyptologist that she has been remembered. The fact that first and last she was a writer of skill and subtlety has gone largely disregarded.

Egypt touched on elements in Amelia Edwards's nature which vibrated intensely. Some of the reasons for this effect are easy enough to identify. First, the monuments of Egypt, the statuary, the reliefs, the paintings, appealed to one who had herself passionately wanted to become an artist. Then there was a sense of recognition, even of familiarity. Wilkinson's *Manners and Customs of the Ancient Egyptians* had strongly impressed her as a child and here she came face to face with a world which had been deeply embedded in her imagination for as long as she could remember. Furthermore, Ancient Egypt offered a combination of two things which co-existed in Amelia Edwards's thought and her practice. She was a romantic novelist in the sense that she made use of unusual, often foreign, backgrounds and sensational events; but at the same time she felt strongly that it was a duty of art to deal with life as it is and not to indulge in free-flying fantasy. Readers should be able to go to books, she thought, and see what life was like in the times when the writer wrote. The sketches she made on her travels exemplify this philosophy, being done with the utmost care for absolute accuracy and without any personalised embellishment. Such recording, made with sensitivity but also with truth, was a function of art she prized highly. The images she found in the temples and tombs of Egypt offered exactly the combination to appeal most strongly to her. There was the romance of the ancient past, with its gods and its profound rituals, and there was also on those walls a record of daily life in the common experiences of men and women in the fields, on the river, or relaxing in their homes.

Even this was not all that Ancient Egypt offered to Amelia Edwards. It challenged and invigorated her enthusiasm for pursuing knowledge and it had the special attraction that it gave scope for individual discovery. Since Champollion had found the key to the reading of hieroglyphs in 1822, great advances had been made in archaeological knowledge but there was still much to find out. Amelia and her party themselves discovered to their delight a hitherto unknown chamber cut in the rock at Abu Simbel: Ancient Egypt, unthinkably old as it was, could still be newly explored.

To convey the excitement and the wonder of all this was the task of Amelia Edwards, the writer. One ingredient of her success is her control of the pacing of the intellectual journey. She has much information to impart and some novel views to put before her readers but she is careful to acclimatise them gently to the atmosphere of her book. Amelia and L. go to look at the Pyramids at Gizeh before embarking on the dahabeeyah but at that stage they are not able really, as Amelia says, to see them. To look is nothing: to see is to bring knowledge and experience to bear and the long journey to come will be a process, recorded step by step, of learning to see. This process begins at Sakkarah with a discussion of the dating of the platform pyramid and Amelia, invoking her reading in the best authorities of the time, leaves no room for doubt that sightseeing is to be taken seriously. At the same time she understands perfectly that the aid of the familiar is required to ease understanding of the strange and the alien and is happy to provide it, as when she suggests the dimensions of a sarcophagus by remarking that "four persons might sit in it round a small card-table, and play a rubber [of whist] comfortably".

Such concessions to a middle-class imagination in no way reduce her commitment to thorough and precise description and discussion. To "see" Egypt is to be required to learn, as she frankly states at the opening of her chapter on Rameses II:

The traveller is ill equipped who goes through Egypt without something more than a mere guide-book knowledge of Rameses II. He is, as it were, content to read the Argument and miss the Poem...As for Abu Simbel, the most stupendous historical record ever transmitted from the past to the present, it tells him but a half-intelligible story. Holding to the merest thread of explanation, he wanders from hall to hall, lacking altogether that potent charm of foregone association which no Murray [the vade mecum of nineteenth century travellers] can furnish. Your average Frenchman straying helplessly through Westminster Abbey under the conduct of the verger has about as vague a conception of the historical import of the things he sees.

Vergers of the late twentieth century, instructed by the tourist industry in all the techniques of promotion, will no doubt repudiate any application to them but the point in essence is a fair one and it underlies all Amelia's accounts of the ancient sights, not Abu Simbel alone.

She urges her readers to be prepared to acquire knowledge not as a pedantic specialisation but as an aid to understanding and appreciation. Egyptian art and its place and significance in the life of the past is, she stresses from the beginning, a subject of utmost interest in itself. That it is also of immeasurable value in widening the mental horizons of the modern visitor is a point everywhere implied. Egypt pushes history back until "one's imagination recoils upon the brink of such a gulf of time", it sets questions of life and death in a perspective unfamiliar to nineteenth century minds and it urges visitors from western Christian societies to stretch their minds to acknowledge other ways of thought by which a society - a great society - lived and flourished millennia before the Christian era. It is not Amelia's way to preach but it would be a very unintelligent reader who failed to see the point.

Her attitude to Egyptian religion is of particular interest. From the time of one of her earliest encounters with it in the Serapeum she takes it seriously: "one cannot but come away with a profound impression of the splendour and power of a religion which could command for its myths such faith, such homage, and such public works". Abu Simbel fills her with wonder and with awe:

Wandering to and fro among these sculptured halls, like a shade among shadows, one seems to have left the world behind; to have done with the teachings of the present; to belong oneself to the past. The very Gods assert their ancient influence over those who question them in solitude. Seen in the fast-deepening gloom of evening, they look instinct with supernatural life. There were times when I should scarcely have been surprised to hear them speak - to see them rise from their painted thrones and come down from the walls. There were times when I felt I believed in them.

Sir Wallis Budge, Keeper of Egyptian and Oriental Antiquities at the British Museum, wrote that he had "never met anyone who had so thoroughly absorbed the mystic and magical influence of Egypt past and present". This at first glance is a surprising comment on one whose major emphasis in *A Thousand Miles* is on history and archaeology but there is enough evidence of her respect for Egyptian ideas and ideals to substantiate it. What Harriet Martineau admired as the "serene and abstract conceptions of the deity" which she found in Egyptian tombs and temples impressed Amelia Edwards too and as with her predecessor it tinged her attitude to Christianity - though this seems always to have been critical. Her account of the religious history of Philae is equivocal: Christianity came and supplanted the old faith; on the "Holy Island" where Osiris had been worshipped in the highest degree of sanctity a basilica was built and the land once zealously protected became home to a large and miscellaneous community; little rude brick dwellings sprang up all over and round the temple, their inhabitants sleeping as soundly at night, Amelia supposes, "as if no ghost-like, mutilated Gods were looking on mournfully in the moonlight". Yet, she goes on: "The Gods are avenged now. The creed which dethroned them is dethroned." Islam drove out the Christians and only a few mementoes remain to show "that Christianity once passed that way".

It was not Christianity alone which sounded the knell of the old Egyptian faith for the faith itself had become corrupted. As she contemplates the Ptolomaic temples of Edfu and Denderah, Amelia's quizzical scepticism asserts itself. The hidden meaning of the legends of the gods had been lost by that time but priests continued to perform rituals which, lacking inner meaning, had become ludicrous. What did the worshippers think of it all, she asks? Did they really believe all these things, or were any of them tormented with doubts of the gods? "Were there sceptics in those days, who wondered how two hierogrammates could look each other in the face without laughing?" Harriet Martineau's Middle East tour persuaded her that all religions fade and fail at last, including Christianity: Amelia Edwards may have agreed with her.

The make-up of *A Thousand Miles* consists of many strata, some, like the passages above, of particular interest for the insight they allow into Amelia's private thoughts. To stress the intellectual or any other level at the expense of the rest risks misrepresenting the character of the book as a whole. Amelia's judgement of the speed at which she can take her readers is combined with her sense of when and how to vary the mood. So an awestruck description of Karnak is followed by an entertaining chapter of incidents involving several encounters with modern Egyptians. One is the Bey of Erment who insists on giving to the Little Lady a ring of his which she has admired:

> It was the way in which the thing was done which made the charm of this little incident. The grace, the readiness, the courtesy, the lofty indifference of it, were alike admirable. Macready in his best days could have done it with as princely an air; but even he would probably have missed something of the Oriental reticence of the Bey of Erment.

That episode contrasts in its turn with the story of a fellah who comes to sell scarabs. He swears that they are genuine "anteekahs" but Amelia knows they are not. To tease him she says that it is imitations she is really after as they are more serviceable for ordinary wear whereupon he assures her that his goods are imitations and, pressed as to when they were made, he adjusts his tale to whatever he thinks his customer wants. Amelia is neither indignant nor contemptuous in the face of this transparent mendacity. Instead it leads her to reflect on her impressions of the Egyptian fellah which she has gleaned from plentiful contacts:

> He steals a little, cheats a little, lies a great deal; but on the other hand he is patient, hospitable, affectionate, trustful. He suspects no malice, and bears none. He commits no great crimes. He is incapable of revenge. In short, his good points outnumber his bad ones; and what man or nation need hope for a much better character?

To many contemporary readers this must have come as a startling thought in contrast to the hostile and prejudiced accounts given by many Nile travellers with minds less open than Amelia Edwards's.

Most conspicuous among the elements of *A Thousand Miles* is the scene painting. During the long stretches when the boat made painfully slow movement or none Amelia studied all that lay before her with minute attention, taking an artist's delight in colour, contour and composition. She painted many water-colours but she also developed verbal reproduction of these pictures to what becomes itself a fine art and to many of them she adds another ingredient, movement. A favourite technique is to list the features of a scene and set each item in action, frequently using the present tense to add to the sense that it is all passing before the reader's eye. Before

50

the camcorder, words did the trick and had the advantage, if the writer had skill and sensitivity enough, of adding the precious element of personal vision. When Amelia describes a street scene in Cairo, out of all that is offered to view she chooses to focus on the colourful appearance of a lady clad in garments of pink, white and black who rides along on a large grey donkey, his legs and hind quarters painted in blue and white and pale yellow; it is she who notices especially the native Sais, or running footman, who "flies" before the carriage of an Egyptian gentleman "wand in hand, bare-legged, eager-eyed, in Greek skull-cap and gorgeous gold-embroidered waistcoat and fluttering white tunic". Like a painter adding shadow to a painting, she adds a touch of tragedy to the bright scene: these Sais, "strong, light, and beautiful, like John of Bologna's Mercury, are said to die young. The pace kills them".

When the scene is a quieter one, active verbs animate it as in this description of a ride through the countryside:

> Along this road, the country folk are coming and going. In the cleared spaces where the maize has been cut, little encampments of straw huts have sprung up. Yonder, steering their way by unseen paths, go strings of camels; their gawky necks and humped backs undulating above the surface of the corn, like galleys with fantastic prows upon a sea of rippling green. The pigeons fly in great clouds from village to village. The larks are singing and circling madly in the clear depths overhead. The bee-eaters flash like live emeralds across our path. The hoopooes strut by the wayside.

On board the *Philae* as on other boats all but the most exceptional must have been bored in dreary hours when the only view was an unchanging and unspectacular landscape; but for readers of *A Thousand Miles up the Nile* nothing is allowed to be dull. There is always something to be pointed out and life and energy never fail.

A Thousand Miles up the Nile was not published till 1877, a time-lag for which Amelia apologises in her preface to the first edition. She spent two years preparing it. Egyptology had not then been brought into academic order. There were certainly none of the aids to research that there are now and she had to find her facts in rare books or scattered far and wide in scholarly journals. To check on a date or a name might take hours of searching. For help with hieroglyphic inscriptions she turned to Samuel Birch, the then Keeper of Egyptian and Oriental Antiquities at the British Museum, and spent hours in his room at the Museum talking to him and learning from him. Birch is said thoroughly to have enjoyed these sessions when Amelia would expatiate to him on "sunrises and sunsets, and the subtle differences of appearance which the monuments exhibit at different times of the day". She could enrich him with her artist's perceptions but what she wanted and gained from him was access to the solid knowledge which he possessed. Others also contributed and she herself worked with her usual unquenchable enthusiasm to dot every i and cross every t. By the time of the second edition in 1879 she had absorbed the scholarly background even more thoroughly as the increased number of references in the footnotes indicates, including some to personal correspondence with distinguished authorities.

The battery of artistic, literary and intellectual skills brought to bear upon *A Thousand Miles* makes it undoubtedly Amelia's *chef d'oeuvre*, the culmination and justification of her years of study and practice, but it did not so much mark a triumphant stage in her career as turn it in a new direction. She would write only one more novel, for Egypt was from now on to take over her life.

Untrodden Peaks had been a fine and original book but it lacked what *A Thousand Miles up the Nile* has, commitment to a purpose. There lingers over *Untrodden Peaks*, for all its interest and charm, an air of self-indulgence. The affair of the saddle and the discomforts of the maid cause uneasiness in the reader and in Amelia Edwards herself because, after all, the ladies are only amusing themselves, using their money and position to play in a world which is real and hard enough to others. In *A Thousand Miles* the situation is different. Exploring the Ancient Egyptian sites is a serious matter, not merely because Amelia has been commissioned to write a book but because as she looks and studies there develops an increasingly powerful sense of mission and responsibility. "The work of destruction goes on apace", she writes as she observes how much has deteriorated even in the few months between her passage up the Nile and the return journey down to Cairo; "There is no one to prevent it; there is no one to discourage it". She has found her task. Henceforth she will put all her energy to galvanising forces to arrest that destruction and her book, entertaining, amusing and also substantial in its studies of history and art and the life of the past, will pave the way for the sustained campaign of the rest of her life.

III   1882-1892: Triumph and Disaster

In 1882 the Egypt Exploration Society, until 1887 known as the Egypt Exploration Fund, was founded in London. Its purpose was to promote and finance excavation in Egypt and it owed its inception to the "energy, enthusiasm and zeal" of Amelia Edwards, as Wallis Budge noted.

Amelia had been deeply moved by the monuments of Ancient Egypt and correspondingly distressed by the irresponsible neglect and despoliation which were adding daily to damage and loss. Egyptians had long helped themselves for their own purposes to the work of their ancestors but since Napoleon and his *savants* had shown the world what riches lay along the banks of the Nile the pace of destruction had rapidly accelerated as buyers and dealers arrived in rapacious numbers. Individuals vied with each other in building up collections of antiques and governments made it a matter of national honour to acquire prize items for their museums. Local Arabs, meanwhile, happily fed the market with their robberies. Acquisitive greed was not limited to easily portable objects. Statues and obelisks were removed, larger items being dismembered if need be, reliefs were taken from walls and the astronomical ceiling at Dendera was cut out wholesale. The tale of rivalry, intrigue and skulduggery has its amusing side with some feats worthy of Raffles, at least in ingenuity , but it is a basically unedifying story and the damage done by a combination of only-too-active predators and official neglect was likely in a short time to become disastrous.

The thrill of the chase always has its attraction and Amelia tells how in early days in Egypt she herself hunted bargains like the rest, the fact that carrying off Egypt's heritage was illegal only adding spice to the shopping. Some moral ambiguity adhered to the situation, as at one time it did in relation to the Elgin marbles, since there was no doubt that the objects shipped away to big museums elsewhere were better looked after than they were likely to be in Cairo. The solution was gradually evolved: excavations needed to be conducted responsibly and expertly, arrangements for the disposal of the finds, acceptable to the Egyptian government and fair to the excavators, had to be agreed and the enforcement of laws forbidding exports without permission of the authorities had to be tightened up. Since money and kudos were involved none of this came easily.

The Egypt Exploration Society (E.E.S.) was founded to make a start on a programme which would be both protective and exploratory. Amelia could not forget the losses being sustained daily nor the "brown mounds" which she had seen all over Egypt and which concealed who-knew-what treasures of papyri and artefacts and larger objects, all likely to be lost or ruined if nothing was done to examine and safeguard them. She personally contacted influential people and secured the interest of the press. The scale and persistence of her efforts were such that she was telling no more than the truth when she wrote to a correspondent years later: "As for the Egypt Exploration Fund, I suppose you know that it was really myself who originated it". Once launched, the E.E.S. recruited archaeologists, sponsored annual excavations and published reports. It continued, mainly through Amelia, to seek to rouse public interest and by doing so gather support and secure contributions. To capture attention sites connected to Biblical narrative were selected for the first dig. The historical credentials of the Bible were coming under particularly heavy fire in the second half of the nineteenth century and an expedition designed to look on the spot for evidence which might authenticate Biblical history was guaranteed to create interest. The gambit worked well. The first sites uncovered by Edouard Naville generated controversy as well as excitement and as a result the E.E.S. was launched in a burst of useful publicity.

The initiative which set the whole enterprise in train and the determination and perseverance essential to carry it forward were alike due to Amelia Edwards. R.S.Poole, at that time Keeper of the Department of Coins and Medals at the British Museum gave her his support but Samuel Birch, Keeper of Oriental Antiquities, was unsympathetic. Birch was not convinced that Egyptian art could stand alongside classical in importance and at the same time he was reluctant to support a scheme which gave the Egyptian government first call on the excavators' findings. Amelia's personal relations with Birch were pleasant but he dismissed her ardent crusade to save Ancient Egypt as "sentimental archaeology". The official attitude of the Museum remained a thorn in her flesh as it later became in Flinders Petrie's. Amelia ensured when she made her will that the Chair of Egyptology which she endowed should not go to any of its employees.

Poole held fast, however, and Amelia exerted all her energy and her personal persuasiveness to recruit other supporters. Important among them was Sir Erasmus Wilson, a distinguished and wealthy surgeon with a known interest in Egypt. Amelia had worked with him on his book, *The Egypt of the Past,* which was published in 1877 and it was he who had met the expenses of transporting from Alexandria the obelisk now standing on

Amelia Edwards as a young woman. The prominent placing of her left hand and the ring on the fourth finger suggest that the photograph may belong to the period of her engagement. (Pl. 1)

Lucy Renshawe, Amelia Edwards's companion on her Dolomite tour and also in Egypt. (Pl. 2)

Dahabeeyahs on the Nile. (Pl. 3)

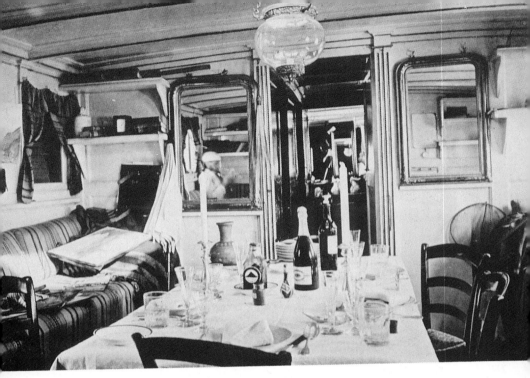

Comforts of life on board a dahabeeyah. The left hand mirror reflects someone in another part of the cabin. (Pl.4)

Sailors from the 'Philae' painting coffee on the face of one of the colossi at Abu Simbel. The idea was to cover patches of plaster left by a previous traveller's cast. Amelia Edwards was amused by the episode and her sketch of the scene includes herself working at her easel under her sunshade. (Pl. 5)

Amelia Edwards's study in The Larches, Westbury-on-Trym. (Pl. 6)

Amelia Edwards at the time of her American tour, 1889-90. (Pl. 7)

Amelia Edwards's grave in Henbury churchyard, Bristol, with its obelisk and ankh. (Pl. 8)

the Thames Embankment and known as Cleopatra's Needle. He became President of the E.E.S. and gave it generous financial aid during his lifetime but to Amelia's great disappointment he left no legacy when he died in August 1884. She was personally saddened also by his death: "I have lost the only companion I had in Egyptological study", she told Mrs Petrie with that rather over-emphatic style she tended to use for personal relationships. Friendships based on mutual interests and common understanding seem to have been rare in her mature years and they loomed correspondingly large in her imagination.

Another supporter who made an outstanding contribution to the success of the E.E.S. was the American clergyman, William Copley Winslow, who became Honorary Vice-President and Treasurer of the Society in the United States. A devoted admirer of Amelia, he worked hard to stimulate interest in the cause and to raise money. In 1889 he stage-managed her American lecture tour and gave her the most conspicuous public success of her life.

The importance of her friendly relations with Wilson and Winslow underlines how much of the weight of the E.E.S. rested on Amelia at its inception and later as it developed. As Honorary Secretary it was she who made contacts and maintained them, with the result that she was immensely well informed about personalities and activities. She was among the first to hear of new discoveries and was able to pass on news and offer advice out of an unequalled store of information. One of her closest contacts was with the French Egyptologist, Gaston Maspero, with whom she corresponded from 1878 onwards. She knew of him through his professional publications and he had read *A Thousand Miles up the Nile*. Literature rather than egyptology dominates the early exchanges between them for Maspero was a keen reader of both English and French novels. He understood how a writer of fiction like Amelia could transmogrify into an archaeologist for, as he told her, archaeology shared with romance the ambition to bring to life the people of the past. He believed that it was the duty of Egyptologists to interest the public, a lesson which Amelia hardly needed teaching and which she always observed with fidelity. She sent him books and consulted him as to why *Debenham's Vow* had been less popular with the public than *Barbara's History*, to which he replied that heroes of novels are required by their readers to be "monstres de fidelité amoureuse" and that Debenham's sacrifice of love for ambition "le rend detestable". It was a surprisingly naive question of Amelia's but the composition of *Debenham's Vow* shows several signs of uneasiness.

By 1880 egyptological matters had supplanted literary criticism in the correspondence and in 1881 Maspero was appointed Director of Antiquities in Cairo. From then on he and Amelia were dealing as co-workers in the field of Egyptian archaeology, concerned with finance and the need for wary handling of relations with the Egyptian authorities.

In 1882 Egypt was experiencing the crisis precipitated when Ahmed Arabi led a revolt which the Khedive's government was too weak to suppress. The job was done for him by the British who then assumed virtual control. It was an unsettled and unsettling period but the concern of Egyptologists at all times was predominantly with the personalities of the officials responsible for antiquities. The mutually involved but often disparate interests of the Egyptian government, foreign excavators and the Director of the museum (then at Bulaq, later in Cairo) made for tension at the best of times but when national feeling was more than usually aroused the situation called for particularly delicate handling. This is a point made emphatically to Amelia by Gaston Maspero. Amelia was inclined to support the appointment of Heinrich Schliemann to excavate in Egypt on behalf of the E.E.S. but the idea filled Maspero with alarm. Schliemann's work in Troy had given him a high reputation but discretion, Maspero warned, was not among his virtues and he had given offence in Turkey by his love of publicity and controversy. In the current Egyptian situation, Maspero writes, an imprudent word or a slip in the manner of presenting a case could cause ministers and officials to refuse permission to dig. He asks Amelia to make it clear to the E.E.S. that permission to excavate is an act of grace on the part of the Egyptian government and some flattery and the greatest patience and tact are called for. Amelia paid heed and Schliemann was not appointed.

The Egyptian situation in 1882 called for special sensitivity but the clash of competing aims and ambitions was neither new nor exceptional. The record of jealousy, self-seeking and stabbing-in-the-back among distinguished Egyptologists must rank high even in the annals of academic rivalries. Among this turbulence Amelia cultivated an expertise as mediator and soother of fevered male egos without which it would hardly have been possible for work to continue and prosper.

Flinders Petrie was one of her protegés. He became the most distinguished archaeologist of his day but at this time he was only a young man of promise, some twenty years Amelia's junior. She recognised his potentiality before others did and took pains to foster a career which might have foundered but for her care and diplomacy. A man of immense energy and total commitment, Petrie expected as much from others as he gave himself and had no patience with those who seemed to him dilatory or neglectful or less seized with the importance of the work he was doing. He respected Amelia but Poole was joint Honorary Secretary of the E.E.S. with her and Poole's methods of working were anathema to Petrie. Finally in 1886, exasperated beyond further endurance, he resigned from the

E.E.S. but not without first trying to persuade Amelia to bring the dispute into the open and herself to campaign on his side and against Poole. This put her in a dilemma. Petrie's gifts as an archaeologist were invaluable to the Society but Poole was "a really dear friend" and she was sincerely attached also to his family. "I cannot bring myself", she told Petrie,

> to the heroic sacrifice of the friendship of a family...with whom I enjoy such close and delightful intercourse when I am in London...I am getting on towards the evening of life [she was fifty-five] and I cannot take new people into my heart and I cling to the few - the very few - friends I have.

A correspondent raised the possibility that Amelia at this moment of crisis could have thrown her lot in with Petrie and resigned when he did:

> if you had gone with Petrie all those 'in the know' would have followed you. In Egypt everyone thinks Petrie has been badly used - not by you - by Poole, under whom it was impossible for a genius like Petrie to work.

But it is very unlikely that Amelia would have been prepared to jettison all her investment in the E.E.S. even if she had not been torn between her admiration for Petrie and her personal attachment to the Poole family. As it was she avoided a rupture which might have meant the breaking up of the E.E.S. and she also took care that Petrie's interests were not fatally damaged. She interested a wealthy Manchester business man on his behalf and thus enabled him to continue a brilliant career.

Amelia Edwards's promotion of Petrie is a part of her services to archaeology. It continued when, by mutual agreement, his letters to his mother in which he gave accounts of the progress of his field-work were passed on to Amelia and she wrote them up for publication. The skill of her pen and the publicity she afforded spread knowledge and understanding of his work and the recognition which was finally accorded him was owing in large part to her effectiveness in bringing him and his achievements to the forefront.

One piece of writing in particular stands out. In 1886 Amelia wrote for *Harper's New Monthly Magazine* an account of Petrie's excavations at Tanis two years previously. It was Petrie's first assignment for the E.E.S. and on the face of it an unattractive one. The appeal for the E.E.S. was its Biblical connections which were always likely to attract subscribers but its location in the eastern Delta was reported to be the resort of wild beasts and infested with reptiles and malignant fevers. Naville had first been designated for the work but decided, understandably, that he would rather occupy himself elsewhere. Petrie found the place scarcely more alluring:

> The miserable Arab huts of San first meet the eye... with on one side a muddy stream into which they throw their dead buffalo, and from which they drink, and on the other a swamp full of rotting graves and filth

but he persevered and his dig brought to light the remains of a vast temple and a colossal statue of Rameses II. These were exciting discoveries in themselves but the expedition derives importance also from the fact that Petrie's interest in the smaller finds on the site led in time to one of his major contributions to archaeology, the development of a methodology for properly studying and understanding the significance of such previously disregarded objects.

For Amelia Edwards it was not the health hazards nor an anticipation of triumphs to come which provided the imaginative thrust of her article. The uncovering of the ancient city gave scope to a power she possessed of projecting herself into a scene and realising it with an almost trance-like intensity. It is a gift exercised several times in her novels, as in *Barbara's History* of 1864 in which one passage remarkably anticipates the essay of 1886. In the novel Barbara visits Tivoli and, her imagination excited by the fact of being physically present on a site which she has intensively studied in books, she astonishes her companion by a dazzling description of a scene in Hadrian's Villa as vivid and intimate as though she were personally present in the past of eighteen hundred years ago. Amelia did not, of course, know Tanis as she knew Tivoli but her imagination was well tuned to make the most of what Petrie had to tell and "The Story of Tanis" draws upon precisely the same creative imagination that she gives to Barbara. She envisages a stranger visiting Tanis in its heyday. He sees the great statue, fourteen times the height of a man, witnesses a procession in honour of a visit by Rameses II and participates in the rejoicing and the ritual. Detailed knowledge vivified by powerful historical imagination make this a striking piece of writing. Maspero's comment that archaeology and novel-writing had much in common is here endorsed by a spectacular bravura display.

"The Story of Tanis" was written in the same year that Petrie's dispute with Poole came to a head. Amelia kept faith with Petrie but she also remained faithful to Poole. He did not always reciprocate with equal loyalty. In Petrie's eyes Poole was sluggish and inefficient in his management of the Society's affairs, a judgement with which Amelia later, if not then, came to concur. Poole for his part thought that Amelia had a tendency to be headstrong and rash and he considered it his duty to curb her excessive zeal. On occasion he took advantage of her being based in Bristol and not free to be frequently in London and he put business through without consulting her. This not surprisingly angered her and she was moved to strong protest. The work she had done and continued to do gave her an indefeasible right, she considered, to be consulted on any important matter relating to the Society. Her letter is written in some bitterness:

> I do not see the use of my giving up everything, earnings, time, health and home duties - if I do not have the least confidence reposed in me by the Committee, and am only told of things after they are done.

Poole made some amends after her death when in his obituary notice he ascribed the success of the Society entirely to her but he could never have been unaware of the volume of work she undertook nor of how much the Society owed to her dedication, grace and tact in dealing with others and, not least, her capacity for efficient organisation. She had learnt order and punctuality from her father and just as she never missed a deadline for her editors however pressed she was for time, so she spared nothing to fulfil punctiliously the multifarious duties she assumed as Honorary Secretary.

It was particularly bruising to her that in 1888 a Committee member accused her of having no system for recording and recruiting subscribers and charged that she was making insufficient effort to enlarge the membership. She made a stout rebuttal including, among other evidence, that in 1886 she had written over four thousand letters by hand to recruit members and money. As she told a correspondent, she alone knew the whole history of the subscription list since its beginning in 1883 and was deeply hurt that decisions were now being taken without any reference to her. New arrangements which had been agreed upon she thought would be very damaging:

> I fear that, organised as it is now proposed to organise it, and conducted by those who are likely in future to conduct it, it [the E.E.S.] will scarcely have so prosperous a career before it in future as it has had in the past.

The cost of her dedication to the E.E.S. was always considerable even when ingratitude did not add its special sourness. "I am stupified with tiredness", she wrote once to Poole and in a letter of 1884 to a bookseller she laments that she has no money to buy as she would like. The books which are necessary to her Egyptian work are expensive and take all the money she has to spare. She writes learned articles but they bring in nothing, or next to nothing, and the time she devotes to them means that she has to decline contracts for novels which would bring her in "many hundreds". Yet the price she paid for her allegiance to Ancient Egypt was a voluntary offering and she organised her life round it. Hard work was a compulsion engrained in her nature and, she said, "I live with the pen in my hand, not only from morning till night, but sometimes from night till morning". Her working hours, she went on, were all those when she was not sitting at meals, sleeping or taking exercise. Exercise itself was carefully regulated, consisting of a measured walk in the garden of The Larches, half a mile before breakfast, half a mile after and the same repeated in the evening. In such a life there was little time for visitors and birds did duty as "intimate friends", a joy to Amelia in Westbury as the Nile birds had been to her in Egypt.

No degree of regulation could quite eliminate disturbance. Mrs Braysher was old and subject to illness and on one occasion a servant was ill at the same time. Amelia sent a hastily scribbled note to an editor: "This is dreadful and I am in great difficulty to get on with my work". Nevertheless, she assures him, she will submit her copy on time. The financial situation grew no better and Amelia began to take on lecturing engagements even though, in November 1887, she was writing to Mrs Petrie: "I am deadly tired - I think I never was so persistently tired in my life". In the same year a secretary, Miss Emily Paterson, was appointed to give her some assistance with E.E.S. work but it was too late to save her from developing that winter what was apparently a serious and protracted illness.

Recovery was slow and perhaps never complete. She reported to Mrs Petrie in the following September that:

I have I think, almost, if not quite, recovered my physical strength. I can walk as well as ever - though I am perhaps rather more tired afterwards; and I can eat and drink anything as before. But my head is not as serviceable as before my illness. My work tries and tires me a good deal, and I find I go to bed with a headache, and get up with a headache always. It goes off after I am up a little while - but I certainly cannot work with as much impunity as of old.

She had been up to London but it took too much out of her. Fortunately a new friend and helper had appeared on the scene, Kate Bradbury, member of a Lancashire family noted for its avid pursuit of intellectual interests including egyptology. The Bradburys indeed, one commentator noted, had been seized by what he called "a fearful outbreak" of egyptological fever. From the same circle came the business man, Jesse Hawarth, whose aid Amelia had secured for Petrie when he left the E.E.S.

Kate Bradbury was to be Amelia's invaluable support and companion and in 1888 she bore her off to the family home at Ashton-under-Lyne where she recuperated from the exertions of the London visit. She stayed in Ashton for ten days and so, she tells Mrs Petrie, "I was not away from my dear friend here for very long".

II

She was soon, however, to be away from Mrs Braysher for far longer. In 1889 she was invited to undertake a lecture tour of America and the prospect stimulated her physically and mentally to the extent that her old vigour and zest returned in force. She was to receive recognition and acclaim in America unmatched at any other time in her career and the tour, which lasted through into 1890, became nothing short of a triumphal progress.

The original idea came from William Copley Winslow, long-time admirer of Amelia and energetic worker on her behalf in the U.S.A. He spared no effort to ensure that she would have a good hearing when she came, writing personal letters to over two hundred prominent people and issuing a leaflet signed by, among others, John Greenleaf Whittier, James Russell Lowell and Oliver Wendell Holmes, in which "the intelligent and cultivated people of our land" were urged to attend her lectures. Ill health put behind her, she entered upon the tour with confidence. She had found that the role of lecturer suited her and the American tour abundantly confirmed that indeed it did. "She addresses her audience with entire self-possession and ease of manner", *The New York Independent* enthused and its reporter was struck particularly by her humour. He assured his readers that study and personal knowledge informed all she said but, he remarked, "even on the platform" she could not resist "giving more or less play to her inborn pleasantry, which gives so much flavour to her conversation". Audiences rejoiced in the unexpected pleasure.

Amelia's voice, trained in youth when a career even in opera had seemed a possibility, was a great asset and it entranced her American audiences. Her instinct for acting enabled her to present herself to maximum effect and her artistic talents contributed their quota as she quickly sketched a hieroglyph or illustrated on a board some point of comparison between Egyptian art and Greek. She gave in all some hundred and twenty lectures to universities, colleges and learned societies in centres including Boston, Philadelphia, New York, Baltimore and New Haven.

Academic America had already paid tribute to her work by the award of honorary degrees, including an LL.D. of the University of Columbia in 1887, but what bowled over the elegant and distinguished audiences who crowded the lecture theatres to hear her was the charm, grace and unpretentiousness with which she laid before them the fruits of her scholarship. The personal impact was such that reporters were drawn irresistibly, if not with entire consistency, to describe her. She is of middle stature, one wrote, and has "a most unusual countenance, clear and fair, delicate in feature ...lit up by the brightest of eyes, and qualified by a mouth of most mobile expression". "She is a tall, fine-looking woman, with silvery hair" and "kindly gray eyes", according to another. A third announced that "she is rather a small woman" with "black hair tinged with gray... Miss Edwards does not look her age". A fourth stressed the appearance of strength in her countenance: her face evinces "great power of self-control", her eyes are "keen gray; the chin firm". Whatever they saw, they liked. This learned lady was neither pompous nor hectoring. She was delightful: she was feminine; and in Boston in particular the women received her as a sister and a model. The reporter for *Boston Saturday Evening Gazette* of December 7th, 1889, was sour on the subject. "For some reason the edict went forth that the English lady was to be the fashion, and, as a matter of course, her success was assured", he sniffed.

> It has been a subject of some wonder that so many Boston women had made a profound study of Egyptian art, and had been waiting for years for such a course of lectures! Nothing could be more absurd than much of the balderdash talked about art by many of Dr Edwards' attentive auditors; but, in Boston, one may as well not exist as not to be up on the topic of the hour...Miss Edwards has been fortunate,

he concludes patronisingly,

> in meeting almost every one of literary and social importance, and has been entertained in civic as well as aristocratic circles.

Irritation at fashionable lionising and affectation of culture is fair enough but there is an additional anti-female sting in this, some of whose venom may have been derived from an event which had taken place eight days previously.

On November 29th, the New England Women's Press Association had given a grand reception in honour of Amelia. The women of the Press Association were feminist in their activities and their aspirations. Brought together only five years previously, they encouraged each other to look for financial independence and the enlargement of horizons and influence that they hoped newspaper work would give them. The arrival of Amelia in their city was an event they delighted to honour for she came not only as Egyptologist, novelist, travel writer, lecturer, artist and, as their chronicler exuberantly puts it, "in short the most learned woman in the world", but also as a fellow-journalist. The reception was arranged on a lavish scale. Two hundred of Boston's most distinguished citizens were presented to her and so long was the line and so eager were the guests to pay their respects that the so-called breakfast, scheduled for twelve noon, was served an hour late. The white and gold colonial dining room of the Parker House hotel was massed with plants and flowers and so also, it appears, were the tables. Nevertheless there was room for five courses, including, for dessert, Gelée à la Cairo. Menus for the guests, topped with a portrait of Amelia, were printed on broad, delicately tinted satin ribbon but for Amelia herself there was a tiny landscape of the pyramids and the sphinx with a decoration of lotus buds and flowers, all hand-painted on creamy white satin ten inches wide. This menu is preserved among the Amelia Edwards papers in Somerville College, Oxford.

There was much speech making. Amelia herself spoke of the opportunities offered to women in the newspaper world and compared England and America in this respect: in America, she found, women were given wider scope than the reviewing and similar roles to which they tended to be confined in England. She ranged from the usefulness of acquiring competence in shorthand, more widely practised in England than America, to a vision of a day when the influence of women journalists would so enlarge the traditional female role of peace-maker that they might be able to help in "crushing down the great crime of war". She regretted that England lagged undoubtedly behind the United States in at least one respect - that it had no provision for women's higher education comparable with Vassar, Wellesley and Smith, colleges which had greatly impressed Amelia when she visited them. She may have had in mind the long and painful struggles which were taking place at home to gain acceptance of the intellectual aspirations of Girton College, Cambridge, struggles with which her cousin, Matilda Betham-Edwards, was well acquainted through her close friend Barbara Bodichon née Leigh Smith. Socially aware as she was, Amelia urged also the creation of industrial and trade schools : if America were to lead the way she believed England would follow.

There was probably no one among Amelia's hosts that afternoon who did not, at least momentarily, call to mind memories of another English writer whom they had welcomed to their city. Some fifty years earlier Charles Dickens had been an honoured guest but in the American chapters of *Martin Chuzzlewit* he bit the hand that had fed him, to the outrage of his hosts all over America. In November 1867, however, he had returned to Boston and stayed in the same Parker House where Amelia was now being fêted. This time he was received with even greater enthusiasm than before, all animosity being forgotten and his reputation soaring to stratospheric heights. The days when Fanny Trollope and Harriet Martineau and Dickens himself could cause an Atlantic storm by their reports of an uncouth society were over. For Amelia Edwards, certainly, all was amity. On arriving, she told her hosts, she found she could scarcely distinguish an American from an Englishman in appearance, manner or education. She had learned, she says, to love the American accent in Rome "where she had learned also that when she met an American she met a friend to whom she offered her hand with her heart in it". It may be thought that her hyperbole does more credit to the quality of her acquaintance and her warm-hearted response to it than to her powers of observation, usually so minute, but in this post-Civil War era she was doing her bit for national and international harmony: "She felt she need not ask to have the friendship between England and America preserved, since they were already so nearly one". The "sin of slavery", as she calls it in *Debenham's Vow*, had been exorcised and she saw nothing now to stand between peoples so nearly allied.

No doubt she also had in mind, as always, the value of the dollars our "dearly beloved Americans", as she calls them once to Poole, might be persuaded to disburse.

Certainly Boston in 1889 left nothing undone or unsaid in its tribute to Amelia. The Parker House event included the reading of a poem by one Henry W. Austin hailing Amelia as a queen and a pioneer - a queen by virtue of her gifts and her learning and a pioneer in that by her achievements she extended "the woman-sphere":

> Yes, by such lives laborious
> Is quicker shapen the plan
> Of the day, when woman glorious
> Shall arise: arise victorious -
> No longer the slave laborious,
> Or the tempting toy of man!

Amelia's vision of women's contribution to world peace may well have been inspiring to the Women's Press Association for they had already in their sights a potentially effective social role. Austin envisages the emancipation of women as leading to the righting of at least one other wrong, the "present industrial slavery" by which the labour of children was exploited. Amelia's reference to trade and industrial schools, sincere in itself, would have chimed well with her hosts' thinking.

The visit to America marked the zenith of Amelia's career. One croaking voice did indeed make itself heard and was to continue for some time to give Winslow anxiety. A Mr Cope Whitehouse was waging war against the E.E.S., impugning both its scholarship and the probity of its principal figures, including Amelia. Time had to be taken during the tour and afterwards to counter his accusations and minimise potential damage to the financial benefits which it was hoped would accrue from the lectures. Whitehouse's animosity, a sufficient irritant at the time, was, however, as nothing in comparison with the final disasters. In Columbus, Ohio, while she was stepping down from the podium after a lecture, Amelia fell, causing a compound fracture of her left arm. She was towards the end of her tour and with her usual iron-willed determination to fulfil her obligations she insisted on continuing with the lecturing schedule in spite of the injury. The pain was acute and on several occasions she had to retire briefly from the platform before she could continue. Two or three weeks later in New York her arm was reset. On the same day she fulfilled three engagements at the last of which, after ten o'clock at night, she delivered an impromptu speech of some twenty minutes' duration in response to a challenge on a point she had previously made. (Perhaps Whitehouse was the challenger.) According to Winslow, who reports this event, she was "unhesitating, clear, fluent, forcibly humorous". On the voyage home the arm was again hurt when she was flung across the cabin by a lurch of the ship. She had yet another bad fall after landing. Doctors told her it would be a year before she ceased to feel the effect of these accidents and she herself doubted if she would ever regain the full use of hand and arm.

The third fall may have caused a bone to splinter and pierce an artery but this, if true, is not the whole story. Kate Bradbury, friend, confidante and amenuensis, had been with Amelia in America and in January 1893 she wrote a letter to two sisters, Alice and Edith Kingsbury, with whom she and Amelia had stayed in Connecticut. She describes how in July 1890 Amelia became aware of something wrong with her left breast against which her wrist had been broken. She saw a consultant who diagnosed incipient cancer and she was operated on two days later. Whether or not the whole breast was removed, the operation was in its immediate purpose successful. "The dreaded evil never returned," Kate Bradbury wrote, "but," she added, "the loss of blood, and the nervous exhaustion, and the shock - she never recovered from."

Revelation of her innermost feelings had never been Amelia Edwards's style and she guarded to the last her right to reticence. She gave instructions that no one was to know of her operation and she went on working, assisted by Emily Paterson on E.E.S. business and by Kate Bradbury who was constantly with her.

Kate Bradbury did all she could to relieve Amelia of distress and strain and it was with her help that Amelia was able to bring out a book based on the American lectures. In *Pharaohs, Fellahs and Explorers* the lectures are recast to accommodate large additions, notes and references. The latest discoveries are included and the width and depth of Amelia's knowledge of her subject are given appropriate scope. This last effort to promote the cause of Ancient Egypt typifies Amelia's dedication and her refusal to spare herself while there was work still to be done but it lacks the distinctive qualities of her earlier work. Lectures intended for one kind of audience and recast for a wider and anonymous public rarely if ever make a satisfactory book and there is no reason to suppose that *Pharoahs, Fellahs and Explorers* would have been an exception even if the conditions of production had been favourable. As it is, the book serves a purpose as a source of information and discussion and from time to time the tone and manner of the Amelia Edwards of earlier days can be heard and seen; but such moments only draw attention to the overall absence of the old sparkle.

In spite of her weakness and need for rest Amelia continued to give lectures during the winter but from March to August 1891 she was abroad again. The journey was evidently made in search of health but it nearly proved fatal. Amelia was so ill in Naples and Rome that it seemed doubtful she would ever come home but, moving further north, she began to improve and in Switzerland progress continued rapidly. "Fog, snow, frost, rain and thunderstorms, did me miraculous good!" Amelia wrote in November to Edith Kingsbury in her old vein of ironic humour: "Ordered to a warm climate, I all but died in it - escaping to a frozen region, I recovered. So much for the doctors." She returned to Westbury and Kate Bradbury had hopes that all would be well. She was not seriosuly alarmed even when Amelia contracted influenza, caught or exacerbated when she supervised the dispersal of a shipment of Egyptian antiquities at Millwall Docks; but the weakness of the past eighteen months had left her without the physical resources to fight it and she died on April 15th, 1892. Mrs Braysher, in her late eighties, had picked up the influenza germ and died of it just three months earlier.

It is too late now for thorough diagnosis of the ultimate cause of Amelia's death, whether cancer or some post-operative complication or some long-seated trouble which combined with general debility to kill her. There are records of several bouts of illness in her life, including the mysterious "pressure on the brain" of 1871 and the illness of 1887 which lasted months and caused severe headaches. Kate Bradbury's account of her last days is, in any case, a grim one, not least for what she has to say about home life with Mrs Braysher at this period.

Amelia's references to Mrs Braysher are invariably full of affection. In May 1884, at the height of the Gordon of Khartoum crisis, she wrote to Poole lovingly and amusingly of her companion of many years. "Old ladies and babies are bound to be vegetables", she began. "My old lady is a most rampaging, vehement, political, belligerent, Gladstone-hating boiling-over vegetable - quite uncontrollable and unmanageable. But in truth", she goes on, "she and I are both heart-sick and exhausted with indignation and impatience and shame at the whole Gordon-Khartoum affair". The picture this suggests of a harmonious relationship based on sympathy of temperament and attitudes is an attractive one. By and large it may have been true of most of the years that Amelia and Mrs Braysher spent together but the account Kate Bradbury gives of the late years as she saw them casts a different and dismal light on the relationship. "Mrs Braysher", she wrote,

was 86, and very trying, and extravagant, and money to keep up with her demands was more and more needed if there was to be any peace at the Larches...Miss E. went on lecturing: she liked it, it brought her change, and absence from the Larches which Mrs B. did not resent, and some money.

It would be wrong to read back from the cantankerous, exorbitant ways of an eighty-six year old a story of bad behaviour stretching back over years but Kate Bradbury's picture of miserable life at The Larches in 1889 does recall features of earlier years which, with hindsight, may be seen as a warning. The "rampaging, boiling-over vegetable" of 1884 was evidently a woman of strong even aggressive views fiercely expressed. Matilda Betham-Edwards tells a story which adds more colour to the picture. An Englishman had got into the bear pit at Berne and been mauled to death. "This occurrence took place", she writes,

whilst I was a guest of my cousin, the late Amelia Blandford Edwards, then residing at Westbury-on-Trym with a friend, Mrs Braysher by name, a woman of much spirit and wit and a passionate champion of the animal world; she had, moreover, lately visited the famous bears of Berne. As she read *The Times* to us at breakfast - the report of the bully and his reception by the unoffending animals, she dropped the paper and sighing deeply, ejaculated 'Pretty dears!'

A passionate champion indeed.

Given good health and temper on both sides such a companion may be stimulating and enjoyable but Mrs Braysher's were not personality traits for all seasons. The aggressive quality which Matilda notices perhaps led her to demand an unreasonable degree of attention and behind Amelia's frequent references to her inability to be often in London we may be hearing Mrs Braysher's vociferous complaints. In 1889-90 Amelia had been away for months, intensifying whatever resentment Mrs Braysher harboured. Amelia's laments about shortage of funds are also highlighted by Kate Bradbury's words.

That money was an issue indicates rather surprisingly that the older woman was dependent on Amelia. Mrs Braysher was the householder, as census reports show, but Amelia was apparently the provider, at least in later years. If this was understood from the beginning it would mean that the prospect of secure financial support for the future formed no part of Amelia's motives in taking up joint-housekeeping in the first place. It is possible that Mrs Braysher had originally had money and had lost it or frittered it away but in any case the remark about her extravagance gives a new edge to Amelia's confession in 1884 that money was tight and it sharpens her comment that Egyptian work brought her next to nothing, whereas novels would earn her hundreds. Perhaps Mrs Braysher's reproaches echo in her words on that occasion and also in the letter to Poole in which she counts her sacrifices for the E.E.S - "earnings, time, health and home duties". If home duties did not consist exclusively of attention to Mrs Braysher that must have accounted for a large part of them. Did Mrs Braysher feel herself neglected, excluded from the all-embracing occupation of the woman she had looked to for life-long companionship? Did the demands of Egyptian work pinch the household budget? If so, perhaps she had some excuse for being "trying" and improvident in advanced old age. Kate Bradbury saw only the bad behaviour but Amelia may have felt that some of the blame lay with her. Hence the painful bite of her question to Poole: had she made sacrifices not only on her own account but also on that of an unwilling other, only to be disregarded by fellow-workers in the very cause for which the sacrifices were made? It is a bitter question and may have many resonances but, whatever the stresses and strains of life together, her attachment to her old friend never really wavered and Mrs Braysher's death in January 1892 added to the misery of the last months.

Amelia's will, like the last twenty years of her life, was devoted to promoting the cause of Ancient Egypt. She endowed a Chair of Egyptology at University College, London, the first such Chair in the United Kingdom, and she made sure by the terms of the bequest that the appointment would go to Flinders Petrie. Her books and her collection of antiquities also went to the College where they are housed, as she directed, in a room dedicated to her. Amelia's support for women's education and women's rights in general led her to choose University College as the beneficiary because the college was the only University establishment at that time to admit men and women on equal terms. She bequeathed her personal papers to Somerville College, Oxford, a women's college with whose Principal she was friendly.

Petrie went to Westbury to help Kate Bradbury sort through Amelia's Egyptian collection and on the Sunday of his visit the two of them went to Henbury church. Mrs Braysher and her daughter Emma were buried in the churchyard and Amelia herself was to lie in the same enclosed space. It was perhaps then and there that Petrie and Miss Bradbury decided that a large stone *ankh*, the Egyptian sign of life and immortality, should be placed on the spot as a fitting memorial. She had worked to restore to life an ancient past: it was right that one of its most potent symbols should accompany her in death.

IV   Amelia Edwards and Fiction

It is regrettable that Amelia Edwards's fiction has been prematurely and unjustly discarded. She is entitled to an honourable entry in the ranks of minor Victorian novelists who are acknowledged still to make pleasurable reading and who illuminate preoccupations, problems and aspirations which remain familiar in the late twentieth century. Her novels have a further claim to attention for the part they play in the development of her mature style, a style which becomes truly a work of art - art of the kind which conceals art. *Untrodden Peaks and Unfrequented Valleys* and *A Thousand Miles up the Nile* show that style in its highest development. Its quality has ensured their survival but no one hitherto has looked in detail at the stages on the way to the accomplishment they represent: the journey is a rewarding one revealing many places worth a stop and many scenes to contemplate and enjoy.

Amelia Edwards's last novel, *Lord Brackenbury* was published in 1880 and in it she made her farewell to fiction. Some twenty years earlier she had proclaimed her faith in the importance of the novel as a literary form and expressed her view of what it should aim at. The ideas are put into the mouth of Hamel, the bogus clergyman, adventurer and escaped convict of the novel *Hand and Glove*, who often, in striking symbiosis, is spokesman for the young Amelia Edwards. His nefarious career is not at this point suspected and he has just impressed and delighted a French provincial evening party with a display of one of his many accomplishments. He has sung to his own accompaniment a passionate poem of frustrated love (written, of course, by Amelia Edwards) and he goes on to speak with special energy and enthusiasm about novels. It is not customary, he acknowledges, to treat fiction seriously but those who dismiss it as trivial are wrong: "Novels frequently embody the highest truths of life, and novelists...labour for something more than the amusement of their readers". They introduce experience to the inexperienced and they remind the world-weary of the ideal. Even more than that: "a good novel is a work of art, and as deathless as a canto of Tasso, or a statue of Michael Angelo".

This is challenging enough to those who believe that fiction is but "the bubble of an hour" but he becomes more heterodox still. The novel of contemporary life delights us, he says, because its scenes and manners are familiar but when time has moved on and other habits and interests prevail it will then be valuable "as a record and authority" preserving the life of generations past. The most interesting works of the Middle Ages are, he declares, the *Canterbury Tales* of Chaucer and the *Chronicles* of Froissart and it is only to be regretted that other great writers

> were so careless of the commonplaces of their time. Consider - had Petrarch and Spenser written novels depicting the life and manners of their respective centuries, how gladly we would have excused the sonnets of the one, and the epic of the other!...what these books would have been to us, the works of George Sand and her European contemporaries will be to our descendants!...In their pages the manners of our day will be enbalmed long after we ourselves have passed away.

Hamel's interest in literature is not exclusive. He speaks with enthusiasm of George Sand's *Adriani*, a now forgotten book concerning a singer whose talent makes him the equal of even the highest born, and he recommends it as a penetrating account of the life, needs and rewards of the artist in any form, whether musician or other. Several references testify to the influence of George Sand in this novel. It belongs to the time of Amelia's life when she frequented artists' studios in Paris, smoked cigars and perhaps wore trousers and when the writings and behaviour of George Sand were part of the atmosphere of the circles she moved in. She could not have escaped the impact felt on both sides of the Channel of the flood of ideas released by George Sand's agency, ideas which overwhelmed the barriers of convention and overturned the canons of respectability. How far in doing so they were liberating and how far demoralising became a keen question. It is raised in *Hand and Glove* when Hamel lends a book to Marguerite and Charles, her cousin and fiancé, comes upon it. Shocked beyond measure at what he finds, Charles proceeds to tear it up page by page. "Heaven forbid," he cries, "that you should see life as he [the author] depicts it, or seek to see it". (Amelia perhaps amused herself by imagining Charles to be misled by the Christian name: he would have been even more scandalised to find that the disgraceful author was a woman). Hamel, when he comes next day, "easy, brilliant, and ready-witted" as ever, takes the affair lightly with

> a jest at the expense of too-virtuous critics, a frank admission of certain minor inconsistencies, an elegant eulogium on one or two fine passages taken at hazard from the mutilated leaves.

Promoter of the claims of the novel as a form of high art and a record of human life and history, Hamel dismisses the narrow-minded morality which would insist on shackles and blinkers and deny the novelist's right to take all experience as his (or her) province.

Amelia's views of the novel at this time are ambitious and radical. One at least of the early objectives that she set is accomplished in the years to come: her novels do undoubtedly offer vicarious experience from which her readers could learn much of the life, manners, history and topography of continental Europe, to say nothing of the educational benefit to be derived from the discussions of art, literature, music and a host of contemporary topics with which her books are packed. The scope and variety of the subject matter she took into her books is their defining characteristic for good or ill and both plus and minus qualities are well illustrated by the first of her novels she published, *My Brother's Wife* of 1855.

Most conspicuously the story gives notice of Amelia's penchant for melodrama, the sort of material which gives some justification for counting her among the so-called "sensation" novelists of the period. It is a highly seasoned mixture of sentiment, murder, adultery and, finally, a wretched suicide but all this is laced with solemn, not to say pedantic discussions of Italian poetry from Dante to Leopardi, the merits or otherwise of Carlyle and an analysis of Beethoven. *My Brother's Wife* overdoses the reader on every item in its range but in doing so reflects its author as she evidently was at this time, a young woman eager for adventure and drama in her life and filled also with excitement at the intellectual and cultural pastures open to her to explore. Given freedom at home to read widely and encouraged to develop her mind and imagination, her enthusiasm for knowledge was uncurbed and inexhaustible. The reviewer of *The Globe* was puzzled, as reviewers of later novels would be, that all this should come from a woman. If it were not for the author's name, he writes, he would take the book to be the work of "a young man who has travelled, read, and experienced more of life, in its widest sense, than the generality". Amelia was encouraged to believe she had found a good formula - a basis of exciting action on to which the riches of travel, art and learning could be poured unstintingly for the benefit of her readers.

My Brother's Wife reads to-day as the crudest example of what was to be Amelia's abiding urge to use the novel as a hold-all, a generous receptacle for all the goods she had to put into it, whether they were, as here, a melodramatic scene treated with relish, a piece of erudition scrupulously developed, or an intimate and loving description of a landscape. The format of the three volume novel is notorious for having forced Victorian novelists to expand their books beyond due length but when Amelia for the first time adopted it in *Barbara's History* of 1864 it represented a happy release. She now had the room she wanted for all the ideas, interests and information that filled her mind and which she longed to impart and she was able to space out the various elements rather more acceptably than in *My Brother's Wife*. She never attained in her novels, however, that judicious balancing and harmonising of different components which she so skilfully and successfully achieved in *A Thousand Miles up the Nile*.

Wide as her range was and especially surprising for a woman of her time, its limits are self-evident. In *Hand and Glove* she makes some moves towards exploring sexual passion, and even daringly hints at its existence in a young girl, but she takes them no further. What was acceptable for the French George Sand was not acceptable to the English audience she needed to reach in order to earn her living and she could not entirely repudiate Charles. He is ignorant and bigoted whereas Hamel is a connoisseur; but fundamentally, as in his comments on the book, he is amoral and morality requires that Charles win Marguerite in the end. Hamel has to be killed off but not before he has left his mark. All in all, his major place in the novel and the respect with which he is treated deserve to be registered as a daring attempt to introduce some (diluted) measure of Sandean freedom to middle-class English drawing rooms.

Melodrama was acceptable to the Victorians and Amelia was always ready to supply that. Passion was not and after *Hand and Glove*, with one exception, Amelia eschewed it. *Half a Million of Money*, a novel of 1865, contains a character called William Trefalden who falls prey to the same driving and ultimately self-destructive yearning that Hamel had for Marguerite. Trefalden is, in fact, another version of Hamel, a clever man, impatient with the restrictions of his status in life and seeking some better outlet for his greater than average gifts. Like Hamel, he can see only illegal means of achieving this. He becomes a swindler and callous manipulator of others for his own ends. Hamel has the advantage of being introduced when his most unscrupulous activities are safely in the past so that the glamour of his appearance and the brilliance of his gifts make their impression without evidence of tarnish. Trefalden, however, is shown when his nasty machinations are in full spate and the greed and malice of his nature are exposed in action. He is, like Hamel, a consummate actor, his act being that of a very likeable, even lovable and sympathetic man. By this performance he wins the confidence of a mother and her daughter, intending to exploit them; but he falls in love with the daughter. It is essential at a late point in the story that he leave the country to save his skin but the girl's mother is dying and she will not leave her mother's side. Trefalden, acutely aware of the danger threatening him, chafed, he wearied, he burned to be gone - but in vain; for he loved Helen Riviere - loved her with all the depth and passion that were in him; and so loving her, could no more have left her in her extremity of grief and apprehension than he could have saved her mother from the grave.

The delay is fatal to him. There is time for the up-standing young hero, Saxon, to disabuse Helen about Trefalden's true nature and Trefalden, denied sight of her, loses all self-control and, wild with grief and frustration, dies in despair. There is no sense of waste at his death as there is in Hamel's but in the grip of an irresistible passion even Trefalden acquires some tragic stature. His love for Helen Riviere defeats his own interests and for once in his life his ruthlessly selfish character yields to care for someone else.

Amelia Edwards is less equivocal in her attitude to him than in her response to Hamel but in both she shows a fascination with characters endowed with superior intelligence and a heightened capacity for powerful feeling and she is prepared to set aside moral judgement so far as to sympathise, even to admire. Hamel and Trefalden may have the Byronic hero and Emily Brontë's Heathcliff in their ancestry but their careers of villainy are pettier than the one and spelt out more explicitly than the other; their redemption through passion, partial though it may be, is all the more striking.

In the character of Hugh Farquhar, the hero of *Barbara's History* (1864), Amelia attempts a combination of the gifted but corrupt "villain" with the incorruptible hero. If Emily Brontë's influence had some part in the creation of earlier figures, it is Charlotte who stands behind Farquhar for he has close affinities with Rochester. A much-travelled, widely experienced man of the world, he has in the course of his peregrinations picked up an Italian mistress. The affair is over but he acknowledges some responsibility for her and houses her in the upper rooms of his ancestral home. When he marries Barbara, his young bride soon begins to see dark shapes flitting mysteriously through rooms and non-existent doors are heard to open and close. All is revealed, repentance and penance follow, Hugh is chastened and forgiven and domestic bliss will, it is to be hoped, ensue.

Hugh is endowed with even more talents than Hamel. He displays an encyclopaedic knowledge of every subject which arises directly or tangentially. He is accomplished in everything, including dancing, singing and shooting. He has a quotation or a cultural reference to suit every situation for ever in his mouth. He has a shady past but he is not criminal. He can be saved by the love of a good woman and so morality and the spice of the slightly wicked can be partnered for the maximum entertainment and edification of the reader. The book was a considerable success and The *Morning Post* was unrestrained in its praise:

> She [Amelia Edwards] has the strength, without the rudeness, which marked that memorable book *Jane Eyre*...Her greatest success is in the perfect delineation of a male character.

What he calls the "rudeness" of *Jane Eyre* was the capacity for passion which Harriet Martineau so much deplored in Charlotte Brontë, the same capacity which, when she allows it, enlivens Amelia Edwards's early novels. In emasculating her later heroes Amelia could hope for readier acceptance but at the expense of making her heroes complacent, preposterous and tedious which, *pace The Morning Post*, Farquhar is. Though he has some guilt to expiate, there is little tension between the upright man and wrongdoer aspects of his character and the dramatic possibilities of the Hamel/Charles situation, for example, are quite lost.

In *Half a Million of Money* incorruptible hero and gifted but corrupt villain are again decisively split off. By contrast with Trefalden, Saxon, the young hero, is ostentatiously *sans peur et sans reproche*. He is given an interesting background but is otherwise a mere stick with nothing to characterise him but his priggishness.

After this second variation on the theme of interesting villain and upright but tedious hero and the attempt to meld the two in Farquhar, Amelia chooses a different tack. Her males are from now on distinguished not so much by temperament as by the world of adventure which they inhabit. Very adventurous indeed some heroes become. They participate in duels, fight alongside Garibaldi's men for the liberation of Italy or go blockade-running in the American South. In a last spectacular flourish, Lord Brackenbury abandons his inheritance, fakes his own death and is metamorphosed into an Italian sailor. With so much activity there is less emphasis on character potential though in *Debenham's Vow* (1870), the first of the new style, questions of character do arise and sit most uncomfortably with the robust and brilliantly handled blockade-running episode.

Debenham's Vow is based on a theme which runs through several of these novels, the frustration and ambition of a character who feels himself cheated of his proper station in society. Hamel and Trefalden take to crime to compensate for lack of means and status; Debenham, brought up in humble circumstances, learns in early adulthood that he is descended from minor nobility and vows that he will restore the family to its "rightful" position at whatever sacrifice to himself or, incidentally, to others. He obtains an introduction to a businessman who, on the strength of a brief interview, sends this utterly unqualified young man to Southern Italy to salvage a ship which has run aground with its cargo off the coast of Calabria. Debenham promptly leaves the life he has known so far, Islington, his mother and his job as parish organist, and proceeds to discharge with decision and the utmost efficiency all the commercial, diplomatic and personal business involved in carrying out this assignment in a foreign country. Since Amelia Edwards details all this as though such transactions were her own meat and drink, the novelty of the setting and the details of the various activities make sufficiently interesting reading for the implausibility of the hero's transformation to be temporarily ignored.

Excited by his success in Italy, Debenham becomes a hard-headed and audacious adventurer and there follows the most remarkable of all the scenes in which Amelia presents an occasion or an episode with such confident familiarity and delineates every detail of event and circumstance so sharply that she might almost be thought to be in the grip of hallucination. She had a powerful visual memory and a powerful synthesising imagination. She spared no pains to gather facts and then she brought them together in a vividly dramatised picture, most astonishingly in *Debenham's Vow* when the hero runs the Northern blockade to fetch cotton from the American South during the Civil War. The social and business life on shore, the nautical manoeuvres when Debenham is under threat both from Northern ships and a violent storm at sea - all the sights and sounds and stresses of dangerous and dramatic enterprises are described as though Amelia herself felt and saw every moment of them. As usual her preparation was impeccable. She had consulted maps and pictures, studied charts and bills of lading, talked to officers and sailors and in general so familiarised herself with circumstances and situations that when a reviewer sneered at what he assumed to be her woman's ignorance of seamanship an Admiral leapt to her defence saying that he would vouch for every word of her account.

All this is finely done but disbelief in Debenham as a character can no longer be suspended when he returns to England, marries Claudia for her money, falls prey to what would now undoubtedly be diagnosed as psychosomatic illness on his wedding-night and lapses once more into the maternal arms, all his gains in money and status being Dead Sea fruit after all.

Amelia may have been prompted to this attempt to conceive the hero's story as moral exemplum by a desire to establish her moral credentials firmly but the result is hardly a success. She was puzzled by its failure and it was still rankling eight years later when she asked Gaston Maspero, Egyptologist and littérateur, for his opinion. She appears not to have realised how the surge of her natural talents in the central portions of the novel militated against the imposed formula of misplaced ambition followed by nemesis; but there are a number of psychological pressures at work in *Debenham's Vow* which derive from the author herself, notably the mother-son relationship and also, it would appear, the resentment at social disadvantage. Throughout her life she eschewed self-analysis and she may have been blind to them.

II

The new role of the hero as man of action is significant in more ways than one for it changes the pivot of the story from a female to a male viewpoint. For the narrator of *My Brother's Wife*, her first novel, Amelia had chosen a man, a natural enough choice and one made by other women writers as a means of breaking out beyond the prescribed boundaries of feminine experience. The same urge motivated the adoption of men's clothing. After *My Brother's Wife*, however, Amelia replaces the male with a female voice and for several subsequent novels a woman's experience and a woman's point of view take the foregound. When the men become adventurous, however, the role of the women diminishes till Winifred and Giulietta of *Lord Brackenbury* scarcely acquire any life at all. Even in fiction a woman's world becomes too confined for Amelia Edwards but before she returns to the male as the conventional centre of action she presents heroines who have character and talent and possess also the courage and initiative to leave familiar environments and travel abroad, alone if need be. Into the mouth of one of them, an intellectual young woman who wins a prestigious prize in a man-dominated field, she puts a bitter indictment of male condescension towards women.

The Ladder of Life is centred upon Natalie but there is too much hectic action going on in this novel for much in the way of character to emerge. Gartha, the narrator and controlling consciousness of *Hand and Glove*, has rather more claim to individuality. As a child she has been deprived of both love and education but on the death of her father and at the age of thirty she goes as companion and English teacher to Marguerite, the seventeen-year old daughter of a family in rural France. Once there she shows herself (against probability) to be a mature, self-confident woman through whose eyes are seen and assessed the various characters who play out their drama. She marries in the end the bear-like and farouche Uncle Alexander and in this, as in some other respects, brings Charlotte Brontë to mind again, this time by way of Lucy Snowe in *Villette*. Marguerite herself is not much more than a child but she begins to grow up in the course of the novel and, as the focus of the attentions of Hamel and Charles she is, of course, central to the plot.

In *Barbara's History* the story is told explicitly as the history of the heroine. It is Dickens who has provided the model here for a *bildungsroman* like *David Copperfield* but with a girl as the central figure. Like David, like Gartha and like so many other fictional children of the nineteenth century - though family life was officially sanctified - Barbara's early years are spent in a cold and unsympathetic home. She is sent to live in Suffolk with her aunt, a Betsy Trotwood figure, and it is there that she encounters Hugh Farquhar, still a young man though some twenty years older than she is. It is not Amelia Edwards's fault that the scenes between the child and the man make uneasy reading nowadays. No doubt his fondling and his lover-like speeches were intended to be nothing but innocent but the underlying sexuality of the relation between man and child, evident enough to modern eyes, adds to the impression of some sexual turbulence in Amelia herself during these years when she moved from her late twenties to early thirties.

When Barbara goes to study at an art school in Germany Hugh follows her and there is occasion for much continental travel in the course of which Hugh gives her in abundance the benefit of his taste and his knowledge. Eventually they marry. Barbara is a talented and spirited girl and marriage does not quench her. When she discovers the Italian mistress she does not hesitate for a moment but instantly, and without giving Hugh time to excuse or explain, she leaves the house with her baby and her old nurse and makes her way to Italy where she supports the three of them by copying old masters. Further trials and illnesses follow before marital harmony is at long last restored.

This then is a novel based on a heroine and it may seem to set a seal on a tendency in the early novels to feminist orientation; but there is an inbuilt anomaly. Barbara shows enterprise and stamina but by and large the medium through which knowledge and experience are filtered to her is Hugh. It is he who knows everything and has done everything. She is the absorbed and absorbent recipient of his teaching. In the end he even supplants her as a student of art, her own aspirations having already been reduced when she became a copyist to make ends meet. Up to a point Barbara is a bold heroine but neither she nor her creator is bold enough to overthrow convention completely and repudiate the role of pupil to the superior male. Yet buried at the centre of the novel is an even greater anomaly, or rather a subversive fact: all the experience and erudition which Hugh displays for the admiration of his willing acolyte comes, in fact, from the woman who invented both him and Barbara. The learning and the experience are hers. It is she, the woman author, who masters the lordly Hugh and overtops him in learning and sophistication. Maybe some young women who read the book found in that something to ponder.

A typical Amelia Edwards heroine is talented and capable of independent and spirited action. As so often, however, Amelia stops short of committing herself unambiguously to a cause or a point of view. She signed John Stuart Mill's petition to Parliament in 1866 but she did not campaign openly for women's suffrage. She read Mrs Browning's *Aurora Leigh* and quoted from it and very likely she knew Mme de Stael's *Corinne* but the painful choice between love and marriage or career does not figure in her heroines' lives. The most overt emergence of feminist themes occurs in *In the Days of my Youth*. The heroine, Hortense, is living alone in Paris supporting herself by teaching. She has literary tastes and has coveted a book in a local bookshop but been unable to afford it. The hero buys the book for himself before he knows of her desire for it but when he discovers her wish he offers it to her as an act of courtesy. Her response is unexpected:

> Do not think me ungracious, Monsieur, she interrupted, if I hold that these so-called acts of courtesy are in truth but concessions, for the most part, from the strength of your sex to the weakness of ours.

> Eh bien, Mademoiselle - what then?

> Then, Monsieur, may there not be some women - myself, for instance - who do not care to be treated like children?

He refers back to the age of chivalry but she rejects alike what she calls "the half-barbarous homage of the Middle Ages" and "the scarcely less barbarous refinement of the Addison and Georgian periods." She goes on:

> Both are alike unsound because both have a basis in insincerity. Just as there is a mock refinement more vulgar than simple vulgarity, so are there courtesies which humiliate and compliments which offend.

Some time later Basil expresses surprise at her knowledge of and interest in intellectual matters and she echoes him bitterly:

> I am a woman...Simply a woman - no more. One of the inferior sex...

> You are unlike every other woman!

> Possibly, because I am more useless. Strange as it may seem, do you know I love Art better than sewing, or gossip, or dress: and hold my

liberty to be a dower more precious than either beauty or riches? And yet - I am a woman!

This is unusually forthright for Amelia and impossible to read as anything other than a direct expression of personal feeling. Whether the burst of rare self-expression was provoked by some particular episode or was an eruption of cumulative anger, clearly it was heartfelt. Yet, as on other occasions where some decisive break with accepted ideas seems imminent, Amelia draws back from a final step. Hortense, who is evidently learned as well as highly intelligent, is awarded a prize by the Académie Française for a poem on Thermopylae but she scarcely expresses pleasure, let alone pride, in this distinction which she might have claimed for her sex as well as for herself. Instead she now places all her emphasis on her "duty" to find her long-lost father. In disdaining public recognition and dedicating herself single-mindedly to the pieties of home and family she recovers, no doubt, the "womanliness" imperilled by her love of art and liberty. A reader shocked by the previous spasm of feminism could be comfortably reassured.

After the marriage which inevitably follows, Basil addresses her as "My wife! my poet!" and makes the late and surprising discovery that he is himself a poet. Possibly some reference to the Brownings is intended but if so it amounts to no more than the slightest of glances in their direction. Once married, Hortense dwindles into a wife and her poetry drops out of sight, whereas Basil with confident immodesty dedicates his new-found talent to serving the world. The reader, as on other occasions, is left to make what he or she can of the curiously mixed signals.

Amelia's habitual refusal to speak out unequivocally on controversial matters may exasperate a latter-day reader but what she offered to her female contemporaries did nevertheless lay down some challenges, in the intellectual content of her novels and in the physical movement allowed to her heroines. Her novels are notably lacking in scenes of conventional English domestic life but they range zestfully over foreign parts. The stifling proprieties of well-bred England were unendurable to Corinne who pined for the greater freedom of continental Europe and to any of her readers who felt similarly suffocated Amelia offered freedom by proxy. Stay-at-homes might at least catch sight in her novels of different lives and wider horizons while for the artistic and the intellectually hungry provision was laid out in generous quantity. She was not a leader in the cause of women's liberation but she helped to feed the hearts and minds of those who had the daring to speak out more frankly and forcefully than she herself ever quite brought herself to do.

III

In the Days of my Youth and *Hand and Glove* are the most intimate of Amelia Edwards's novels. *Hand and Glove* is very early and embodies a daring of thought and action never reproduced later. Amelia was forty-two when *In the Days of my Youth* was published and the title she gave her novel may be a hint that reminiscences of her own life are not far in the background of what purports to be the story of a young man. Her last novel is also revealing but in *Lord Brackenbury* suggestions of personal biography are less striking than the gathering together and development of themes familiar from earlier books. It is also notable for its bravura as if Amelia was determined to make a last display of her capacities and skills before she turned her talents to other fields.

Lord Brackenbury includes for the first and only time in an Amelia Edwards novel the figure of a professional writer, a woman. She is Mrs Pennefeather, the wife of an impoverished clergyman and she writes novels to keep the wolf from the family door. Amelia's wry wit goes into the naming of her: Mrs Pennefeather's motive for writing is money, or pennies, and the weight her productions will bear is - a feather. Her novels, however, are not entirely worthless. "Neither brilliant nor profound", they are "unquestionably amusing and by no means without cleverness." Mrs Pennefeather herself has no inflated view of them but is simply glad, for the sake of authors and circulating libraries alike, that the British public is "providentially blessed with an instinctive craving for rubbish". Such was Mrs Pennefeather's estimate of her own abilities, Amelia comments, "and due abatement made for exaggeration, she was probably not far wrong."

There were a number of women writers among her contemporaries who supported their families by their writings, the immensely popular Mrs Braddon and Mrs Oliphant among them. Amelia neither gained readers on their scale nor practised their facility. She spent two years on every novel whereas they poured out book after book in unceasing production. In characterising Mrs Pennefeather's efforts she may have been aiming at one or more of her sister-novelists but it would be characteristic of her if she meant in quizzical self-disparagement to include herself also as a target. In any event, she seems to have determined on a final display of her particular themes and specialities to give readers the opportunity to make up their own minds as to the quality of the fare she offered them.

Lord Brackenbury pursues not one but two stories with separate heroes and heroines. The heroes are brothers but of contrasting types. Cuthbert, the elder and heir to the peerage, inherits his characteristics mainly from his Italian mother. He hates politics though when he succeeds to the title he will be expected to take his seat in Parliament. The family tradition is

Conservative but his sympathies so far as they go are Liberal. He loves music and the fine arts and Italian literature. He is also addicted to sailing. Lancelot, the younger brother, is a decent young man, a good specimen of his class and untroubled by unorthodox ideas of any kind. Cuthbert, who has no wish to marry and perpetuate the dynasty, is induced as a matter of duty to propose to Winifred Savage, niece of an old friend of his father who later became an enemy because of a law suit over disputed land. Amelia has as usual taken pains to master her subject and she sets out this legal business with her customary enthusiastic thoroughness. Winifred is not much more than a child. She has been brought up to marry Cuthbert and though she does not love him she respects him: the situation is a duplicate of Marguerite's in relation to Charles in *Hand and Glove*. Cuthbert's father voices what were presumably Marguerite's parents' opinions too:

> Girls, you must remember, if well-trained, have really no inclinations of their own. A judicious parent or teacher forms their inclinations in finishing their education, just as a skilful cook adds this or that flavour before sending a dish to table.

The cannibalistic image that this respected member of society uses is shocking, even outdoing in brutality the Prince's father in Tennyson's poem *The Princess* when he speaks of hunting women for the beauty of their skins. It echoes the hints of strong though subdued views on women's rights elsewhere and gives an additionally hard edge to Hortense's word "barbarous" in *In the Days of my Youth*.

The father dies and Cuthbert becomes Lord Brackenbury. His more sensitive nature allows him to realise that Winifred and Lancelot have grown to love each other whereupon he contrives an elaborate charade by which it will seem that he has met with a fatal accident in Italy. This leaves the way clear for Lancelot to succeed to the peerage and to marry Winifred. Attention now focuses on these two. Winifred has been brought up as an orphan by her aunt, another of the fierce but ultimately lovable eccentrics like the aunt of *Barbara's History* who derive much of their pungency from Betsy Trotwood. A naturally energetic and joyous girl she has been taught that "the mirth of a well-bred young woman must never exceed a smile" but nevertheless she retains some spirit. When her aunt dies she takes herself off to Munich to study art, that constant preoccupation of Amelia Edwards's heroes and heroines alike. These scenes also recall *Barbara's History* but as with Basil's late vocation to poetry in *In the Days of my Youth*, it is Lancelot who eventually gains a reputation as a painter. Amelia's attacks on the crude attitudes which are considered socially acceptable are launched with more than usual fierceness in *Lord*

Brackenbury but even here she is not prepared to give her heroine an independent career.

Four years pass before Lancelot and Winifred can allow themselves to be persuaded that they may in good conscience assume Cuthbert's death and are at liberty to marry. Lancelot takes his place as a Conservative in the House of Lords. His brother's doubts about the political system trouble him not at all and he is willing enough to accept the request of his friend, Mr Cochrane, of "the Wax and Wafer department, Downing Street" to be put in as Conservative member for the constituency. There is no question of a contested election. In a letter Lancelot reports with a mixture of disdain and lordly indifference on the manner of choosing a representative: canvassing consisted of calling on half a dozen men and giving them a lunch at which

> Three or four shop-keepers talked bad grammar and the thing was done. He [Cochrane] seems vastly pleased, and has visions of governmental loaves and fishes. At all events, he can 'write himself down an ass' - I beg his pardon; I mean an M.P.

Amelia Edwards could count on contemporaries to remember Dickens's Department of How-not-to do-it and the Eatanswill bye-election but if recalling Dickens gave extra thrust to her satire, the political attitude is undoubtedly her own. She was a radical when she frequented Laurence's studio as one of his phalanstery and thirty years later she is a radical still. Her contempt for the political *status quo* comes out again and again in *Lord Brackenbury*. One character on being told that Cochrane works in a government office remarks that "Those government offices nowadays are little better than genteel idiot asylums", a phrase taken up by the American Countess Castelrosso in the course of an argument on the relative merits of British aristocracy and American democracy:

> We have nothing of that sort - no traditions, you know; not even so many idiot asylums as you have. But then we have no younger sons of noble birth to push through the world. That, of course, makes a difference. In the absence of culture, and traditions and idiot asylums - we look to what a man is...we appreciate brains. With brains, a man may do anything in America.

Amelia's sympathies in the Italian struggle for liberation had lain with the republicanism of Mazzini, as *Half a Million of Money* makes clear. In *Lord Brackenbury* she comes closer to home in this contrast between the British system of inherited privilege and an American republicanism in which brains count for more than birth and cleverness is esteemed, rather than treated with suspicion.

Italian politics themselves are not forgotten in *Lord Brackenbury* and they are even forcibly dragged in most incongruously on the wedding day of Cuthbert and Giulietta, the very young Italian girl whom he has wooed and won in his new life as an Italian sailor - by this time he has prospered to the extent of being a ship-owner and captain of a merchant vessel. The bridal pair are sitting outside the Café Florian in the Piazza San Marco when an Austrian band enters and begins to play. Some of those present get up and walk away. Cuthbert explains to the ignorant Giulietta that he has seen times when every well-dressed man and woman would leave the square:

> Did you never understand, child, that you were born and bred under an alien rule...these Austrians are here as masters...their taxation is simply the levying of tribute money. These very coins with which I am about to pay for the coffee...are badges of servitude imposed upon a subject people.

Cuthbert apologises for allowing himself to get carried away on a subject so unsuitable to a romantic occasion but it is, of course, Amelia Edwards who has insisted on including in her final novel a theme on which she has long felt strongly.

Lord Brackenbury is something of a *tour de force* and conceived as such. Amelia has chosen to demonstrate her novelistic skills by taking two stories, developing them in the main separately but interweaving them tightly at the beginning and end. Cuthbert's dramatic disappearance early on which frees Lancelot and Winifred for their own lives is not fully explained till towards the end when an impostor attempts to claim money from Lancelot. Then Cuthbert returns to England to see the family solicitor and acquaint him with all the facts so that he can dispose of the threat, Lancelot and Winifred themselves remaining to the end in ignorance that Cuthbert is still alive. The programme of the novel, which involves curiosity aroused and satisfaction deferred, movement between England, Italy and France, a large caste of characters and plentiful action, is a complicated one and requires dexterity in the management. Amelia makes sure that her readers notice this by drawing attention to it at the beginning of one chapter. She goes on, with undoubtedly false disingenuousness:

> if it should sometimes seem that incidents and personages 'not germane to the matter' make unwarrantable intrusion upon a stage

already occupied, it must be remembered that life is made up of such intrusions.

Many of these "intrusions", such as those on the status of women and on politics, concern topics which have certainly been preoccupations of her own life. For another, of a different character, she feels she has to make a special excuse.

Crammed as it already is with matter of diverse kinds, for even better measure *Lord Brackenbury* includes towards the end an eruption of Vesuvius. This was an event which Amelia had witnessed in 1872 and it made a deep impression on her. She wrote about it and she lectured in Westbury about it. She could not resist including it in *Lord Brackenbury* though it is out of chronology since the main action of the novel is supposed to take place in the 1850's. "This anachronism", Amelia writes, "will, it is trusted, be condoned in favour of the truth of local colour with which the author, as an eye-witness of the event, is enabled to present the scene". There is a touch of self-indulgence here which is reflected in the novel as a whole as Amelia loads her already elaborate structure with themes which have dominated her life till then. Perhaps it should rather be said that she was clearing her mind of earlier preoccupations so as to concentrate in the future on the progressively engrossing cause of egyptology.

Revelling as in one way she does in such a scene as an eruption of Vesuvius, with her usual capacity for seeing more than one side of a matter she is conscious that the spectator's position is in some degree morally impure. In the novel the Countess Castelrosso considers herself "wonderfully fortunate" to have seen such a spectacle and Amelia on her own account as writer and artist can hardly have thought otherwise. She gives it to Winifred, however, to see things from another angle for Winifred's mind is full of the terror and suffering of those whose lives and homes are endangered by the awful event. Here, as in *A Thousand Miles up the Nile*, Amelia acknowledges a danger she sees at the heart of the artist's pursuit of his art. In the earlier book she confessed with shame how easy it was to be enthusiastic about some picturesque subject and forget that the figures in the landscape were flesh and blood men and women, not lay figures existing solely for the pleasure of the artist. The same point is made here by Winifred whose role in this scene serves in more than one way to diminish the charming and brilliant Countess. The Countess, watching the scene in front of her, elaborates a theory that Dante took the notion of the lowest circle of hell from a Swiss glacier and the fiery circle from an eruption of Vesuvius but Winifred dismisses it as mere "babbling". The theory was almost certainly Amelia's own and perhaps a favourite: but she was moving away from fiction and with it from what she may have come to consider mere intellectual pirouettes. Henceforth authentic records of the past and the tangible evidences of real lives would be her business.

The scene with Mrs Pennefeather turns naturally on the craft of writing but like other scenes in the novel it is made to carry other freight as well and here Amelia allows herself an incidental dig or two at the clergy. Parsons figure prominently in many contemporary novels but are conspicuous by their absence from Amelia's. When they do appear, their paucity in number is hardly offset by their piety. The Vicar of the Pennefeathers' parish is married to a Manchester heiress and he divides his time "pretty equally between travelling abroad and angling at home". The work of the parish is left to Mr Pennefeather whose means are narrow and so is his mind. His hard-pressed wife ekes out the family income with her pot-boilers but he keeps a nervous eye on her work. Ghost stories are popular and bring in the money but he has decreed that she must not include a human apparition in hers on the grounds that "we know nothing about disembodied spirits and should not tamper with such subjects." Mrs Pennefeather is at her wit's end but Winifred comes to the rescue. Why not a story about the ghost of a cat? she suggests. Mrs Pennefeather seizes on the idea and the story is a great success.

This little anecdote has two aspects to it. It ridicules both the smallness of Mr Pennefeather's mind and that of a church which is pernickety about insignificant things while it neglects greater; and it draws attention to Amelia Edwards's own prolific story-making imagination. It is Amelia's fertility of invention which is on display when Winifred so effortlessly solves Mrs Pennefeather's problem. The large number of short stories she wrote - among them ghost stories - are evidence of this gift and so happy is she in the exercise of it that short stories spill over into the novels. Among the often labyrinthine major narratives, independent inset narratives appear quite often in the novels. In fact, Amelia Edwards is at her best with the short span. However slack the structure as a whole, individual units within the novels are likely to be well-handled, vivid and dramatic, engaging the interest and holding it. This gift is depreciated in the *Lord Brackenbury* scene where the triviality of Mrs Pennefeather's work and the restraints which govern it disparage the whole activity of fiction-writing but if Amelia was mocking herself she was at the same time inviting her readers to note the wit and resource with which Winifred supplied at once the germ of a story, absurd as it and the public's taste for it might be. Remembering the success of some of her rivals, she seems to be giving a half-mocking demonstration that she fell nothing short of them in fertility and was certainly not deficient in "cleverness".

Amelia's own ghost stories were among the most successful of the genre and Dickens commissisioned them for the Christmas numbers of his *All the Year Round.* Her apparitions, it goes without saying, are human. The longest and most elaborate of the ghost stories is *Monsieur Maurice,* a novelette of 1873. It is an historical story told with all the loving care for period detail to be expected of one with so acute an appreciation of scenes and the objects within them. The spook when it appears is benign but an atmosphere of entirely human evil is quite chillingly built up. Amelia's ghosts do not suggest that supernatural manifestations were any more than a titillating idea to her, though she was susceptible to the powerful impression made by the Egyptian gods and on one memorable occasion in Abu Simbel, alone in the innermost sanctuary, she was siezed with a most unwonted panic.

That she prepared her novels carefully and filled them to the brim not only with narrative but with the fruits of her reading, thinking and travelling is everywhere apparent. *Lord Brackenbury* was prepared with her usual inexhaustible care as she describes in a letter to Mrs Petrie, wife of the distinguished archaeologist, Flinders Petrie (not yet knighted). Mrs Petrie wrote to Amelia in 1887 after a careful reading of *Lord Brackenbury* and Amelia replied thanking her for having spent time on what she calls "that worthless little book" and responding to her comments. In an avant-propos to the novel itself, she writes as though Cuthbert's disappearance were historically true and she had done research to piece the facts together. Such a claim, a well-known literary gambit, is not entirely misleading in this case since Amelia refers Mrs Petrie to several real-life stories which she has conflated to make "a good plot". As for the Cheshire dialect used by local characters which Mrs Petrie queries, Amelia is confident she cannot be faulted. Cheshire friends, she explains, made a vocabulary for her and, ingeniously, she has invented conversation to fit the words they supplied. Details of the setting are genuine also: the location is Biddulph Moor, the houses are Biddulph Grange and Biddulph Manor. Miss Langtrey's house is Moreton Hall. "I studied all the plans on the spot, and sketched them all," Amelia writes, adding that the large finished drawing she made of Old Moreton was engraved in *The Graphic* where it was attributed to Luke Fildes A.R.A. It was a compliment but it is to be hoped that any fee went to the right address.

The thoroughness of preparation which went into *Lord Bracklebury* was typical. It informed the best passages of Amelia Edwards's novels and gave substance to the rest. She was a serious practitioner of her craft and the individual style of novel which she evolved won admiring readers not only at home but abroad. *Lord Brackenbury*, the most popular of her fiction, went into many editions, was serialised in Australia and New Zealand and translated into Russian, French and German. In spite of this, her novel-writing career has sunk out of sight behind her work in egyptology and her books are now very hard to find. This fact makes a real gap in knowledge of the literary and social world of the nineteenth century just as it militates against a proper appreciation of the talents and accomplishment of an outstanding woman.

Towards the end of her life Amelia Edwards wrote an essay called "The Art of the Novelist" which appeared in *The Contemporary Review* two years after her death. It consists very largely of an historical account of story-telling beginning with the Egyptians and finishing with Thackeray, in her opinion "the greatest master of fiction the world has ever seen". This literary/historical survey has little distinction and the essay as a whole bears the marks of a tired mind. It lacks the snap and vigour of the critical views expressed by Hamel in *Hand and Glove* though Amelia strongly reaffirms the opinion which she has held ever since he enunciated it in 1858. The proper business of the novel, she says again, is to give a picture of contemporary life and she singles out Dickens, Trollope and Thackeray as representative chroniclers of the history of their time. On another point she has retreated. Charles was incensed by what he saw as the impropriety of a book which Hamel had lent to Marguerite but Hamel defended it. Amelia Edwards herself had been impressed by George Sand's opening of new ground in life and art but, by the time she wrote "The Art of the Novelist", what had initially been welcome as liberating freedom now appeared to her unequivocally to have deteriorated into licentiousness. "..in our own day", she writes in 1890, "and not very far removed from our own shores [i.e. in France] there has of late sprung up a depraved school of so-called realistic fiction". George Sand was acceptable at thirty; at sixty Zola was not. Now Amelia insists on the moral function of literature: "The world of fiction", she writes "...is a world governed by the law of poetical justice...it satisfies our inborn sense of right; it transports us to a purer atmosphere; it vindicates the ways of God to Man". Fiction should make "for ideal good, for that Beauty which is Truth, and that Truth which is Beauty". Keats's words which she appropriates are big enough to be capable of all sorts of interpretations but the tendency of Amelia's remarks leans towards the conventionally moralistic and gives a misleading view of her own work. It is true that her novels "end happily" but not without some tension between what is and is not the truly admirable. "Legends, like novels, seldom arrive at a satisfactory ending", said Hamel in one of his penetrating comments but "The Art of the Novelist" has no room for ambiguities and nuances.

The essay begins with a long and enthusiastic account of an Ancient Egyptian tale and what follows is perfunctory by comparison. That she was asked to write as a novelist shows that the public still recognised her in that rôle but to read it now is to see clearly that her own interest had shifted elsewhere. When she left fiction for Egypt she was far from leaving her writer's skills behind. On the contrary; but there was no more fiction after *Lord Brackenbury*.

V   Autobiography - or "as much as the Author chooses"

Amelia Edwards wrote two autobiographical accounts, both of them for American audiences and at the request of editors with an eye to the interest roused by her American tour. One is an article entitled "My Home Life" published in 1891 by the periodical, *The Arena*. It had been agreed that she would be free to write entirely on her own terms with no interviewer to question or prompt her and on the basis of what she calls the "straightforward simplicity" of this arrangement she promises to do her best to present herself "literally 'At Home', and in my habit as I live".

The article begins with a description of Westbury, past and present, before homing in on the house where Amelia has lived for a quarter of a century "with a very dear friend". These domestic surroundings were evidently of a highly unusual kind:

> As soon as the front door is opened, the incoming visitor finds himself in the midst of modern Egypt, the walls of the hall being lined with Damascene tiles and Cairene woodwork...In a recess opposite the door stands a fine old chair inlaid with ivory and various coloured woods, which some two hundred years ago was the Episcopal chair of a Coptic bishop. The rest of the hall furniture is of Egyptian inlaid work.

Curios of all kinds from many parts of the world crowd and overcrowd every surface.

A similarly dense packing of a lifetime's memorabilia is found again in the library. As she works at her desk with her back to the windows, Amelia has before her the tangible evidence of the studies and literary labours of her life. Among the books which stand two or three layers deep on the shelves are those dating from the time when she read the British poets "straight through without a break, from Chaucer to Tennyson". Others recall the work she did for various historical compilations and yet others testify to her devotion to Homer and Shakespeare. Representing the latest of all her tasks and enthusiasms are, of course, the books devoted to Egypt and Egyptian archaeology.

The library reflects other life-long interests also. There are books on the fine arts, collections of engravings and an easel on which to display any one of the many pictures which are stacked round the room ready to be brought out as desired. Casts of antique busts rest on pedestals and, facing each other in an archway, stand a much prized marble torso of a river god, picked up years ago from a London curiosity shop, and a large terracotta amphora found in 1872 in a Roman cellar behind the Baths of Caracalla and bought by Amelia on the spot. The books and the antiquities surround Amelia with both their history and hers and the environment gives perfect expression to that fusion of works of art with the men and women who made them which always unfailingly stimulated her intellectually and emotionally; but there is not much room in it for living presences. It would be difficult to move in this hall or this library without knocking something over; but in fact the danger was minimal for visitors were not welcome. Amelia was too busy to socialise. Any visitor was rare but for the very exceptional there might be the special privilege of a sight of the most prized treasure of all, Amelia's collection of Egyptian antiquities. When Petrie went with Kate Bradbury to sort through these after Amelia's death it was a major task, for little porcelain figures of the gods and the three thousand year old dates, lentils and nuts intended for offerings to them, together with rings, necklaces, scarabs, and pieces of mummy cloth were stowed away all over the house in whatever odd corner could be found for them - the place was "solid" as Kate Bradbury reported.

Amelia's antiquarianism was not squeamish. She had three mummified hands in the library and "the heads of two ancient Egyptians in a wardrobe in my bedroom, who, perhaps, talk to each other in the watches of the night, when I am sound asleep" - an idea to set the nerves jumping. It is a pity it came too late to be the basis for a ghost story but it shows she had not lost her taste for the Gothic supernatural. Her list of human relics leads to one of those shifts in perspective which occur in many contexts in her writing. "Here is a baby's foot", she says, cheerfully, but she adds in parenthesis "(some mother cried over it once)".

The end of the article is in sight and Amelia disingenuously confesses that so far she has described only her home and not herself. To repair this omission she quotes from the columns "of some hundreds of newspapers", in which her "brethren of the press" have presented her to their readers and in which they have contradicted each other in every detail. Her hair is variously coal-black or snowy white or iron-grey and her figure is alternatively commanding, tall, slender and engaging, or of middle height and inclined ("alas!" she sighs) to *embonpoint*. She refrains from confirming or correcting but merely concludes with heavy irony: "As it is obviously so easy to realise what I am like from the foregoing data, I need say no more on the subject". On the topic of her daily life, she is hardly more communicative. There is little or nothing to tell, she says, for it consists entirely of work, continued usually till two or three in the morning and sometimes throughout the night. The concluding paragraph of the essay is a charming account of writing the last words of *Untrodden Peaks and Unfrequented Valleys* in a May dawn just as a nightingale on the pear-tree outside her library window burst into a flood of song.

The reader is left with a glow of pleasure and a sense of having been honoured by informal and intimate contact with a delightful personality. The intimacy, however, is illusory. Far from being an example of "straightforward simplicity", "My Home Life" is as carefully calculated for the effect it is to achieve as anything else Amelia Edwards wrote. A keen awareness of her audience was one of the attributes of a successful writer that she specially cultivated and this essay in all its graceful accomplishment is an object lesson in reader-control. Disarmingly presented as an intimate chat, "My Home Life" is in fact no such thing. Readers are skimmed charmingly over surfaces whose depths they are carefully discouraged from looking into. The life of remorseless seclusion and mental activity is glamourised and stripped of all considerations of health, temper, personal relationships and inconvenient domesticities of any kind. To be fixed, pen in hand, perpetually at one's desk except for the regulated and quasi-mechanical walk along a half-mile path is a way of life, however voluntarily chosen, which cannot but carry penalties and impose strains. Even the yearly visits to Weston-super-Mare, undertaken each summer for the sake of Mrs Braysher's health, were occasions to be dreaded for they exposed Amelia to intrusions which took her away from her work and made her burden all the heavier afterwards. Some of the stress and pain of this way of life are evident from correspondence of these years but nothing is allowed to disturb the rosy picture of "My Home Life". Anything more revealing would have to be looked for between the lines and Amelia Edwards is adept at closing the gaps.

Some glimpses of life beyond the library door are allowed, though they are tantalising in their brevity. She mentions famous names among her acquaintance, Gustave Doré, for example, who gave her a copy of the folio edition of his *Don Quichotte*, on the fly-leaf of which he described himself as "ami affectueux". Amelia had written a little book called *The Story of Cervantes* in 1862. This was no more than hack work and hardly in itself the basis of an affectionate friendship but Doré and Amelia corresponded for many years on evidently familiar terms. Browning wrote a "delightful inscription" for the first volume of *The Ring and the Book* which is on Amelia's shelves: he was one of the original sponsors of the E.E.S. and at least knew of the household at The Larches. John Addington Symonds gave her copies of his work and dedicated *Many Moods* to her. Symonds was Marianne North's brother-in-law and Amelia calls him "a dear friend of many years": she tended always to be lavish with her affectionate epithets and how far in any one instance they can be relied on as a measure of close acquaintance is doubtful. That she knew by correspondence and in some degree of friendship many distinguished men is certainly true and she was proud of the fact, once drawing up a list of the "remarkable" people she knew; but personal acquaintance may not have gone far. In any case "My Home Life" is unexpansive. Here as elsewhere small disclosures do not disturb a larger reticence and they leave uncertain how much or how little lies behind a bare mention.

"My Home Life" is a polished piece of writing, expert and delightful. In form and manner it is quite different from the second autobiographical document, the status of which is mysterious. It exists in manuscript among the Amelia Edwards papers in Somerville College and is in the form of a letter. The first page is missing and with it the date and the name of the intended recipient. It must belong, however, to the same period as "My Home Life" and like the essay it is written at the request of an editor, this time of *The Literary World*. Whereas "My Home Life" is suave and controlled, however, the letter is almost chaotic. It seems likely that its composition preceded "My Home Life".

The Literary World, subtitled "A Fortnightly Review of Current Literature", was published in Boston, home ground of W.C. Winslow, indefatigable promoter of Amelia in America. Volume XX, covering 1889, contained a eulogistic article by him stressing the range of her writing, from learned articles to popular sketches and stories, and the "intelligent vividness" with which she made the far-away subjects of egyptology "as interesting as a sensational romance". Given Winslow's enthusiastic prompting, the editorial requests which arrived at Westbury are hardly surprising but the letter from *The Literary World* seems to have taken Amelia aback somewhat. To provide an article or story was nothing to shy at but this editor wanted biographical material, a "life" with which he could introduce her to his compatriots. This was unfamiliar and uncertain ground. She has nothing interesting to say, she protests, no feat to record, no dramatic mischance : "The life of an author - what is it but a record of copy written and paid for, or not paid for, as the case may be?" Yet, feeling perhaps that she owes it to Winslow to do what she can, she pushes on to give much of the biographical material relating to her early years which has been used in previous chapters of this book.

Arrived at the present and the recent past, she gives a rather more relaxed account of life at The Larches than in "My Home Life", describing her lovingly collected and dearly prized objects merely as "miscellaneous rubbish". She makes a welcome addition to the rather grim picture of her regulated outdoor walks by including ferns, flowers and gardening among her hobbies and she even allows a glimpse of herself lying in summer on a long Indian chair under a shady tree to do her reading and writing. Her delight in birds is again manifest. Having got so far, the embarrassment of the opening lines reappears. All this is quite unworthy of record, she says:

> But it is all I have to tell. I live the life of a cabbage which has not even enjoyed the distinction of getting into a pickle - and what can such a commonplace vegetable have to say of its life and adventures?

Mrs Braysher had once been a rampaging, boiling-over vegetable but Amelia now denies herself so much life as that. This seems a final dismissal of any claims to interest but it is immediately followed by a qualification:

> I do not, of course, imply that I have never mixed with the world and gone into society. I have, on the contrary, done my London seasons, and undergone the usual treadmill of dining, driving, dressing and the rest of it, till I became too weary of the wretched round to submit to it any longer.

At what period and in what circumstances these onerous London seasons occurred she does not say. They hardly seem consistent with the far from affluent family life in Islington but it is likely that they belonged to the early 1860's and owed something to Mrs Braysher's patronage at that time. "I have known many notables, too, and seen many phases of life", Amelia continues and, a little later: "I could write many a chapter on 'people I have met'"

This is not the only hint of stories that could be told but are withheld. In spite of the initial disclaimer of any adventure worth mentioning, she does mention several. She had nearly broken her neck once or twice, she says, nearly shot one of her best friends, been all but drowned once in Italy, narrowly escaped falling over a precipice in the Jura, and she had experienced three earthquakes as well as an eruption of Vesuvius. Dismissing as of no account these various adventures, she nevertheless notes them as she notes her acquaintance with "notables" but will not elaborate on them. Clearly before she settled down to be "a cabbage" at Westbury there has been a period in her life full of vigorous activity of many kinds and some dramatic adventure. Though she is not willing altogether to suppress it, neither will she elaborate on it.

"My Home Life" is not by any means the full and frank causerie it purports to be and likewise the letter, more revealing as it is in many ways, also tells much less than a full story. Refusal to talk about the active years leaves a great gap at its centre. Childhood and early youth are far enough away for fulfilments and frustrations to be treated with honesty, even to the extent of some bitterness at the "wasted years" spent studying music and the half-suspicion that her real vocation had been elsewhere than to literature. Life in the present is a different matter, skated over lightly, not only because of such obvious restraints as the involvement of other people but also because it has its roots in the years she will not talk about. In the letter, as in "My Home Life", the image of a settled, orderly life undeviatingly devoted to work lacks a dimension.

The letter is defaced by a large number of crossings-out and its chronology confused by the insertion out of order of belated recollections. The signs of difficult composition are confirmed at the end when Amelia confesses to her correspondent her acute discomfort in the whole enterprise. She has been working at it, she tells him, "by fits and starts" for nine days tearing up many pages in the process. "The egotism of the whole thing is quite horrid", she writes, "and if I were to read it through again, I should surely burn the sheets in disgust". Though the man to whom she writes is a total stranger to her, she is anxious that he should understand how little congenial this attempt at self-record has been: "Pray believe me", she begs him,

> when I tell you that I never thought so much about myself and my doings before, and that I am not an egoist - however much appearances may this time be against me.

The letter appears never to have been sent. A biographical article for *The Literary World* in 1891 is confined to basic facts, Amelia evidently being unable to bring herself to allow into the light of day a letter which she had forced out of herself with so much reluctance. The contrast with the cool assurance of "My Home Life" is striking and it seems reasonable to suppose that the essay was the later piece to be written. Learning from experience, Amelia's agreement to write for *The Arena* depended on the condition that she would have complete control over the ground to be covered and that she would not be propelled into areas where she did not want to go. In these circumstances she was able to move over her chosen territory with complete confidence, free of the deep uneasiness induced by *The Literary World's* request for the story of her life.

What lies at the root of this uneasiness is the question which inevitably arises and one that Amelia Edwards herself may have been unable or unwilling to answer. A biographer can only deduce possibilities and with diffidence offer suggestions.

"I knew her constitutional tendency to melancholia", Kate Bradbury writes, a startling statement to set against the tributes to Amelia's liveliness of spirit and friendly temper and against also the evidence of *Untrodden Peaks* and *A Thousand Miles up the Nile*, books in which she appears to come nearest to "being herself". Kate Bradbury was a most devoted attendant on Amelia during the last years of her life and spared nothing after her death to fulfil what she knew would have been Amelia's wishes. If anyone understood Amelia it would be she and her words have to be weighed carefully. The roots of the melancholia may or may not be identical with the reason for Amelia's almost panicky disinclination to contemplate the story of her life. In either case the difficulty of identifying them is no less. Melancholia may be a temperamental inheritance, in abeyance possibly in youth and during periods of energetic activity but surfacing in age with illness and loss of physical powers; but an inheritance of this kind would not necessarily preclude self-scrutiny - it might even encourage it. Alternatively, a disappointment or series of disappointments may engender melancholy, disappointment in love being an obvious possibility. Difficulties do seem to have arisen with love-relationships in Amelia's early years but it would need to be a remarkably severe blow to give an indelible tinge to the life of a woman who pursued two careers with vigour and success. Lack of close personal connections may, all the same, offer a plausible explanation of a deep-seated sense of loss or deprivation. If this was true of Amelia the aloneness was itself, it appears, a matter of temperamental choice. "She does not love many people for all her seeming geniality", Kate Bradbury told Petrie, adding that Amelia could list only two or three people for whom she really cared. "Seeming geniality" covering a privately solitary spirit is a plausible recipe for melancholy arising from essential loneliness. The satiric spirit which remained always active in Amelia and her caricaturist's instinct inevitably put some distance between her and those she encountered. Close attachment to her mother and the apparent disorientation following her death also contributed their share, perhaps a large share, to the difficulty of forming other relationships.

Other factors may have contributed to the temperamental cast which Kate Bradbury notes. Amelia's childhood and adolescence were attended by great promise and great praise, especially from the mother, but the early attempts at making a career ended in disappointment. The frustrating of her ambitions in art and the failure of her attempts in music must have been severe blows to confidence and though she succeeded as a writer the burden of early promise may have lain heavily upon her. If she felt that she never quite fulfilled it and that some potentiality remained always unrealised, she could with some justification have looked outside herself for the cause - the fact that in the social climate of her day she suffered two disadvantages, her lack of social standing and her sex.

To consider the implications of social disadvantage for her career and personal life is to get a sharpened understanding of the importance to her of her American experience. She goes out of her way to tell the editor of *The Literary World* that she has long cherished a warm admiration for the American people. "I love them", she says,

> for their ready sympathy, their large generosity, their frank appreciation of excellence wherever it may be found, their chivalry towards women, their warmth of heart and their admirable humour and intelligence.

"Frank appreciation of excellence wherever it may be found" is a key phrase in this. It recalls the conversation between the Countess Castelrosso and Lady Symes in *Lord Brackenbury* and it harks back further to the radical sympathies of the young woman who frequented Laurence's gatherings in the 1850's. Apart from the wider implications it had some personal relevance to Amelia. Matilda Betham-Edwards says that her cousin cherished considerable family pride but the bare fact was that the home of her youth was the straitened one of a half-pay officer and minor bank employee. She earned a little extra money as and when she could and she established herself as a journalist. Thereafter she earned respect as a novelist and enough money to travel but she never became one of an inner literary circle in this country. She chose to spend a large proportion of her time abroad, in part, perhaps, because it was cheaper and also because there she could be accepted for what she was regardless of social background. The award to her of a Civil List pension shortly before she died, "in consideration of her services to literature and to archaeology", was welcome from every point of view but the late recognition at home was no substitute for the more congenial tone of society which she believed she found in America.

Democratic recognition of merit regardless of social background was an idea to appeal to Amelia on several counts. Her praise of American chivalry towards women is a more questionable compliment. When she wrote *In the Days of my Youth* in 1873 she would certainly not have included chivalry in any list of virtues, for the heroine of that novel makes a bitter attack on the patronising superiority which she sees at the heart of it. Amelia might or might not have been surprised to know that the American Winslow, in a generally warm tribute to her after her death, could only say that she was logical "for a woman". Amelia was a supporter of women's suffrage and left legacies to benefit the cause of women's education. She could not fail to see or experience that a relatively humble social background was not the only obstacle in the way of an attempt to raise herself to eminence but that the fact simply of being a woman stood even more inexorably in the way. Marianne North's experience offered an object lesson in the truth of this. Unlike Amelia, Marianne came from a wealthy and influential family and it was her sex not her standing which excluded her from honours. A child in Australia asked her if the Queen would give her a knighthood on her return home in recognition of her valuable work and the Queen did indeed feel that the country owed her some recognition, at least for her generous gift of her paintings and the gallery in which to house them. Regretfully, however, she had to ackowledge that there was no honour within her gift. She gave her a signed photograph instead.

No honours system existed which took account of the services of women. Amelia Edwards and Marianne North would both be well aware of this as of many other forms of discrimination both overt and insidious. One of Amelia's lectures, given in Manchester and elsewhere, dealt with "The Social and Political Position of Woman in Ancient Egypt". In ancient times, she says, women of the Nile Valley were recognised as the legal and social equals of men, if not their superiors, and she draws telling contrasts between their rights and the lack of them suffered by her contemporaries in nineteenth century England. A small but growing band of women attacked the injustices head-on but others, less adapted to the front-line, chose outward conformity for the sake of acceptance and the opportunity it gave them to work for whatever objectives they valued.

Amelia was one of the latter kind. Moral courage, she acknowledged, was not among her characteristics. When it came to a confrontation with the courier in the Dolomites, it was L. who had to face him and despatch him: Amelia shrank from collision. She saw the need for social reform and she believed in women's rights but she stood up openly for no cause - except for the preserving of the antiquities of Egypt. There she took the initiative, campaigned tirelessly and exploited to the full her very effective public relations skills; but the weapons she used were patience, charm and womanly peace-making, nothing to threaten male leadership and kudos. One episode demonstrates particularly clearly the policy she adopted towards her male colleagues. She was the first person to decipher the signs on potsherds found by Petrie in the Faiyum in 1889. Petrie sent her facsimile sketches of the potsherd graffiti and by the next post, as she told Winslowe, she was able to return numerous identifications with Cypriote, Phoenician, Lycian, Theran, Phrygian, Etruscan and other letters, a highly significant finding in the chronology of Ancient Egypt. Whereas a man might have built a reputation from this coup, Amelia made no attempt to put herself in the limelight and corner attention. Instead she kept quiet and, while all about her speculated as to the finds, she held back for Petrie's official report to appear.

Her tact and diplomacy on this as on other occasions were crucial to the success of the E.E.S. and this was acknowledged. Colleagues were fulsome in their praise of such qualities as "her unfailing good feeling and kindly nature, which made enmities impossible" - Petrie, who made this tribute, was in a particularly good position to know. Budge also praised her personality warmly: "She was large-hearted, kind and sympathetic, a delightful companion, and a good friend". There is, however, less emphasis in their comments on the intellectual strength which enabled her, not a trained archaeologist, to master specialist material even to the extent of independent work on the potsherd graffiti and to present papers to the International Congress of Orientalists; or on the self-discipline, skill and acumen with which she discharged the tasks she undertook, or the quality of the writing in which she publicised to the world the work of the excavators. *The Saturday Review* obituary gives a lengthy and judicious account of her work in all its aspects but the patronising attitude commonly adopted to women's work contaminates even this. The writer mixes praise and condescension in revealing sentences:

It is much to her credit that, in spite of strong views on certain subjects, as, for example, on what are called 'women's rights', she never became a faddist...The sweetness of her temper,

the writer concludes,

set an example to many who were intellectually her superiors.

The dismissal of women's rights as a "fad" and the assumption of Amelia's intellectual inferiority reflect attitudes which evidently he takes for granted. Amelia's "strong views" must often have been offended but she refrained from forcing them on her colleagues knowing that her acceptance of their patronage secured their acceptance of her as a fellow-worker and in that role, as she moulded it, she could effectively steer the course of British archaeology. She responded angrily to Poole's attempt to wrest the E.E.S. out of her hands, a clear indication that beneath the pliant appearance lay a firm determination to maintain her *de facto* authority. By 1888 her inability to be often in London had seriously weakened her grip on events there but she still had the power to exert a controlling influence on the future. The terms of the legacy by which she endowed a Chair of Archaeology ensured that it would go to Petrie, the man whom she had singled out from the first as a possible future leader.

The praise accorded her might often smack of condescension to a hand-maiden but she knew that she was responsible, almost single-handedly, for the establishment of Egyptian archaeology as a serious discipline in Britain. In that field as in others she knew her capacities, however well or ill others recognised them, but the effort of sustaining and motivating her way of life might well have become oppressive, especially at the late period when Kate Bradbury saw her constantly. Tired from years of over-exertion and weakened by the recent falls and their consequences she had also to bear with Mrs Braysher whose companionship, once a blessing, had become a burden. "There are worse things to be dreaded even than death": Kate Bradbury's comment on her decision to encourage Amelia to go on lecturing, despite the fact that she knew that she needed rest, suggests that the melancholia had become a serious pathological state.

The consolations of religion do not seem to have played any part in Amelia's life. She was very alone at the end. Kate Bradbury, the last of the female companions who meant so much, served her well but as a junior. She could not replace the mother-figure.

Some of the most perceptive comments on Amelia Edwards are made by William Winslow in an obituary article he contributed to *The American Antiquarian* in November 1892. "Miss Edwards's genius", he writes,

> belongs to the objective rather than the subjective school; and she assiduously cultivated her powers and tastes in the direction of objects rather than subjects of thought, or, if the latter, from without rather than from within...She was searching, investigating...but she lacked at least in her novels, that imperial philosophic element, the subjective insight and genius of creation which permeates and sways the "Daniel Derondas" that are given the world.

Middlemarch, Winslow goes on to say, typifies the "subjective" novel as *Lord Brackenbury*, "so full of life, light, color", in his opinion typifies the "objective" novel.

He puts his finger on a crucial point. Amelia Edwards will investigate anything except her own reactions. This refusal weakens her novels because to venture far into the hearts and minds of her characters involves a degree of self-exposure she will not risk. Her other work blends information, wit, charm and high intelligence in a combination which can be brilliant but stops short of the profound. Some barrier in the conscious or sub-conscious mind prevented her from digging into the depths of herself. What lay there may have been nothing of great moment though to recognise it might have made for her greater ease in her personal life. Self-analysis would not necessarily, however, have made her a better novelist or a better Egyptologist and it might well have prevented the creation of that persona through whom she achieved her greatest results.

The last word should be of success and achievement. Whatever irritant lodged in the recesses of Amelia Edwards's character and however severely at times it chafed her, she created in life, as in her writing, a personality through which she mediated knowledge and understanding, made possible the work of others and stimulated the minds of experts, amateurs and the general public to awareness of a great civilisation which had been lost to sight for nearly two thousand years. To achieve this she worked at her persona and disciplined its presentation in the same way as throughout her career she studied style - "worked at it as if it was a science", as she said. An occasional character in her novels may make an acerbic comment or a few be drawn on caricaturist's lines but such attitudes are kept firmly out of sight in her relations with colleagues and acquaintances. Similarly, in the novels and elsewhere a topic or event may sometimes arise to cause uneasiness about accepted judgements but such issues are not pushed far in her writing and seem hardly to have been touched on at all in life. An edge in the voice can from time to time be heard in the books and a sardonic gleam caught momentarily in her eye but "geniality" was the keynote of the woman who was shown to the world, the "Amelia Edwards" persona which had been developed and honed like a tool and which served its purpose so triumphantly in *A Thousand Miles up the Nile* and in the creation of the Egypt Exploration Society.

Amelia Edwards was an outstandingly gifted woman with a remarkable capacity for controlling her life to extract the maximum quantity of work from it. To appreciate as fully as possible how over the whole range of her activities her gifts expressed themselves and to understand something of how much her talents and her achievements cost her is to pay a proper tribute to a woman who is known at present by only a part of what she was. "My work will, I hope, in a sense go on forever", she told Winslow, at once adding a characteristic qualification: "- in the limited sense of our forever". She had in mind her work for egyptology and the provision she had made for its future and in that context the hope was not extravagant. She did not look for immortality through her fiction, however the definition of immortality might be qualified, but she knew that *A Thousand Miles up the Nile* was in a class of its own. "This is the most important of my books", she wrote, " and the one by which I most hope to be remembered". There follows again the typical retraction: "- if I may hope to be remembered at all!" She should be remembered - for the book which continues to live into our own day, for her services to Egypt and scholarship, and, as a woman, for the courage and effort with which she sought to find outlet for the gifts and energies which pressed upon her for expression. Tensions in her nature caused her pain but she won her measure of pleasure and fulfilment too. She deserved it and she deserves the notice of posterity.

Note : Matilda Betham-Edwards

As the source of the most intimate existing accounts of Amelia Edwards her cousin, Matilda Betham-Edwards, deserves a word on her own account.

She was born in 1836 at Westerfield Hall, about three miles north of Ipswich in what was then a village. Her father farmed a considerable acreage and although there were a number of children it was Matilda who took over the running of the farm when he died in 1864. After some twelve months she gave up the farm and moved to London to devote herself to a literary career which would eventually span twenty five years. She was a copious writer and has a place in the history of the rural novel. The books she wrote about her native Suffolk and its country people are notable for the precise and loving knowledge which informs them. She scorned Hardy for not being as well versed in rural life as she was and for making, she claimed, ignorant mistakes.

Largely self-taught, she was well-read and travelled abroad as a girl to study French and German. She developed a particular enthusiasm for France, the people, the country and the culture, and wrote with enthusiasm and extensive knowledge drawn from first-hand experience about both metropolitan France and French North Africa. She edited the *Travels in France* and the *Autobiography* of Arthur Young, noted agriculturalist and writer, and she was commissioned to bring up to date Murray's *Handbook to France*. In 1891 the French government recognised her services to Anglo-French understanding by making her an *Officier de l'Instruction Publique de France*. She received a gold medal at the Franco-British Exhibition of 1908 and was awarded a Civil List pension by the British Government.

In some respects Matilda was a more conspicuous figure than her cousin. She appears at least to have been assimilated into contemporary society in a way Amelia never was. She was a close friend of Barbara Bodichon (née Leigh Smith) who was renowned as a campaigner for women's rights and as a promoter of higher education for women - she was one of the prime movers in the founding of Girton College, Cambridge. Through Barbara Bodichon, Matilda came to know George Eliot and G.H. Lewes and spent a holiday in the Isle of Wight with them. In her late days when she lived in Hastings, Henry James would make his way up the steep hill to her house to call on her. Sarah Grand, novelist and feminist, wrote an admiring memoir of her.

She herself, in striking contrast to Amelia, wrote two volumes of memoirs and reminiscences and it is very evident that she had none of the reclusive tendencies and reluctance to reveal herself which are characteristic of her cousin. They were similarly radical in politics and disaffected in religion but, unlike Amelia, Matilda had no hestitation whatever in expressing her views in unequivocal terms. After early support for women's suffrage she turned against it, denouncing what she saw as the mean-spiritedness of women, i.e. their failure to give due recognition to distinguished members of their own sex. She made no secret of her conviction that her own deserts were not properly recognised either by other women or the nation at large. As she wrote to Sarah Grand towards the end of her life, "My literary Diamond Jubilee 1857-1918 won't, I fear, bring me my deserts, viz., the title of *Baroness* as accorded to Miss Burdett-Coutts. Any lesser distinction I should refuse ...". It is hard to imagine her cousin ever adopting a similar tone.

Matilda appears to have had some sort of breakdown in 1874 and to have become dangerously dependent on chloral but she got over both the illness and the chloral and lived till 1919. She was only five years younger than Amelia who had died when there was still nearly a decade of the nineteenth century to run. Though she describes Amelia as a girl as "robust", it was evidently Matilda who had the tougher constitution. She had certainly a less subtle mind and character. Up to a point the two cousins mirrored each other as writers, travellers and promoters of a cause, Ancient Egypt for Amelia, France for Matilda, but nevertheless they were very different women. There is no comparison between the quality of their writing. In what she had to say and how she said it, the complexity and artistry of Amelia's work at its best is in a quite different category.

Among the family ties which Amelia and Matilda shared was Matilda's aunt, the god-mother after whom she was named. This Matilda Betham was a well-known miniaturist and also a poet, on terms of close friendship with Charles and Mary Lamb. Matilda wrote an essay about her which prompted Amelia to record her own memories of this figure from the past. In a letter published in "The Academy" in September 1878, Amelia recalls a childhood memory of Matilda Betham and the reminiscence gives the incidental occasion for a fleeting and attractive glimpse of family life in Islington when Amelia herself was a child. "My own recollection of Matilda Betham", she writes, "is particularly vivid. When I was a very young girl, she used to drop in occasionally to my mother's tea-table on a summer evening and charm us with talk about Mme. de Stael, Southey and the days of the great French Revolution

...[Note the adjective.] She generally carried a big basket and a Brobdignag umbrella. From the depths of this umbrella she would sometimes bring out some magazine of many years gone by, and read aloud, with not ungraceful emphasis, a poem of her own ... Her eccentricities of dress were proverbial. My father once met her in a frequented London thoroughfare serenely walking in crimson velvet slippers, and followed by a train of little ragamuffins, to whose 'chaff' she was good-humouredly indifferent".

For a brief moment in these words figures of Amelia's childhood come to life.

Sources

i)   Manuscripts:

Somerville College, Oxford.
Egypt Exploration Society.
University College London, Library.
Department of Manuscripts, the British Library.
The Heritage Centre, Macclesfield.
Record Office, City of Bristol.

ii)   Select Bibliography:

Betham-Edwards, Matilda, "Amelia B. Edwards : her childhood and early life", *The New England Magazine*, January, 1893.
   Mid-Victorian Memories, London, 1919.
   Reminiscences, London, 1903.
Birkett, Dea., *Spinsters Abroad : Victorian Lady Explorers*, Oxford, 1989.
Bowker, R.R., "London as a Literary Centre", *Harper's New Monthly Magazine*, June, 1888.
Budge, Sir E.A. Wallis, *By Nile and Tigris*, London, 1920.
David, Rosalie, *The Macclesfield Collection of Egyptian Antiquities*, Warminister, 1980.
Dawson, Warren R., "Letters from Maspero to Amelia Edwards", *Journal of Egyptian Archaeology*, vol. 33, 1947.
   Who Was Who in Egyptology, ed. with E.P. Uphill, 2nd ed. 1972, Egypt Exploration Society.
Drower, Margaret S., "Gaston Maspero and the birth of the Egypt Exploration Fund (1881-3)", *Journal of Egyptian Archaeology*, vol. 68, 1982.
   Flinders Petrie, London, 1985.
Frank, Peter, *The Rape of Egypt*, London, 1991.
Harper's New Monthly Magazine, vol. 65, 1882 and vol. 73, 1886.
James, T.G.H., *Excavating in Egypt : the Exploration Society 1882-1982*, British Museum Publications, 1982.
Janssen, Rosalind M., *The First Hundred Years : Egyptology at University College London 1892-1992*, UCL, 1992.

Keay, Julia, *With Passport and Parasol*, B.B.C. Books, 1989.

Layzell, Doreen, *Invitation to Henbury*, Bristol, 1984.

Linton, Eliza Lynn, *My Literary Life*, London 1899.

Literary World, The, vol. XX, 1889, Boston, U.S.A.

Lord, Myra Belle, *History of the New England Women's Press Association 1885-1931*, Newton, Mass., 1932.

Macquoid, Mrs. K.S., *Women Novelists of Queen Victoria's Reign*, London, 1897.

Melman, Billie, *Women's Orients : English Women and the Middle East, 1718-1918*, Basingstoke and London, 1992.

North, Marianne, *Further Recollections of a Happy Life*, London, 1893.
A Vision of Eden, Exeter, 1980.

Orr, Clarissa Campbell (ed.), *Women in the Victorian Art World*, Manchester, 1995.

Petrie, Flinders, *Seventy Years in Archaeology*, London, 1931.

Pye, John William, "Painful Last Days of 'The Queen of Egyptology'", *KMT*, 1995.

Robinson, Jane, *Wayward Women. A Guide to Women Travellers*, Oxford, 1990.

Showalter, Elaine, *A Literature of their Own : from Charlotte Bronte to Doris Lessing*, Princeton, 1997 (rev. ed.).

Summers, Montague (ed.), *The Supernatural Omnibus*, Bracken Books, London, 1994 (1st published 1931). Includes Amelia Edwards's stories "The Phantom Coach", "How the Third Floor Knew the Potteries", "The Engineer", "My Brother's Ghost Story".

Sutherland, John, *The Longman Companion to Victorian Fiction*, Harlow, 1988.

The Contemporary Review, August 1894.

Thomson, Patricia, *George Sand and the Victorians*, Basingstoke and London, 1977.

Uphill, E.P. *See* Dawson, W.R.

van Thal, Herbert, *Eliza Lynn Linton*, London, 1979.

Wilkinson, Sir J. Gardner, *Manners and Customs of the Ancient Egyptians*, London, 1878.

Wilson, Sir Erasmus, *The Egypt of the Past*, London 1881.

Winslow, William Copley, "The Queen of Egyptology", *The American Antiquarian*, vol. XIV, Nov. 1892.

Works by Amelia Edwards discussed in this book:

My Brother's Wife, 1855.
The Ladder of Life, 1857.
Hand and Glove, 1858.

Sights and Stories; being some account of a holiday tour through the north of Belgium, 1862.

Barbara's History, 1864.

Half a Million of Money, 1865.

Debenham's Vow, 1870.

Monsieur Maurice, 1873.

In the Days of My Youth, 1873.

Untrodden Peaks and Unfrequented Valleys, 1873.

A Thousand Miles up the Nile, 1877.

Lord Brackenbury, 1880.

"My Home Life", 1891.

"The Story of Tanis", 1866.

Pharaohs, Fellahs and Explorers, 1891.

"The Art of the Novelist", 1893.

Index